Loretta Santini

NAPLES
AND CAMPANIA

Published and printed by

plurigraf

NARNI - TERNI

W9-CHC-318

Photographs: Archivio Plurigraf - Amendola - Sperandei
Aerial photos autorization SMA n°506 del 20-6-91

© Copyright by CASA EDITRICE PLURIGRAF
S.S. Flaminia, km 90 - 05035 NARNI - TERNI - ITALIA
Tel. 0744 / 715946 - Fax 0744 / 722540 - (Italy country code: +39)
All rights reserved. No Part of this publication may be reproduced.
Printed: 1997 - PLURIGRAF S.p.A. - NARNI

Historical notes

The Region of Campania was established in its present configuration in 1861, after the unification of Italy. Previously, its territorial area had variously expanded or decreased in response to historical events, while at the beginning of our century part of the present province of Caserta was temporarily included in the Region of Lazio. Campania comprises 5 provinces (Naples, Avellino, Benevento, Caserta and Salerno and borders on Lazio and Molise to the north, Apulia to the east, and Basilicata to the south. Campania represents the fusion of various important geographical regions. The most significant of these is the Campanian region proper, the ancient "ager campanus" (from which it derives its name) which, from remotest antiquity, had its principal centre in the town of Capua. Further inland, the more mountainous area known as Samnium was occupied by the Samnite people and in part by one of its constituent tribes, the Oscans. Another ancient tribe, the Irpini, gave their name to the territory of Irpinia, which roughly coincides with the province of Avellino. Another area known as the "Land of Work" (the medieval "Terra Laboriae") corresponds to the coastal plain of the province of Caserta. The Campanian territory was largely inhabited in prehistoric times, as may be deduced from the discovery of archeological remains, including weapons and household utensils, scattered over the whole region. At the beginning of historic times the area was occupied and settled by Italic peoples, particularly by the Oscans, who long held sway over the more mountainous and inland territory of Campania. Simultaneously, another civilization, that of Greece, put down roots and flourished in the region; a series of Greek colonies was established along the whole littoral and, within a relatively short space of time, attained great cultural importance and economic prosperity. Naples, Pompeii, Paestum, Cumae and others were all cities of Greek origin which expressed fully the civilization of the country by which they had been colonised: in society, in customs, in thought and in art. The Etruscans, too, inhabited the region, displacing the Oscans and diffusing their

splendid civilization. In the 5th century B.C. the whole region fell into the hands of the Samnites. They continued to dominate it until the arrival of the Romans (273 B.C.), to whom, nonetheless, they put up a tenacious - and for a long time successful - resistance. The Romans vanquished and the history of Campania was henceforth inseparably linked to the destiny of Rome: Its life, culture and economy enjoyed the greatest prosperity. "Campania felix" - as it was then called - was appreciated and admired for its heritage of Greek culture, for the fertility of its soil and above all for its natural beauties which led emperors and other illustrious Romans to build sumptuous villas in the region's most enchanting resorts. Upon the fall of the Roman Empire (5th century AD.), Campania was overrun by barbarians on several occasions, and eventually reduced and occupied by the Lombards (in the 6th century AD.). The Lombards established the Duchy of Beneventum, its territorial extension successively eroded by the secession of various towns, including Amalfi, which became the first maritime Republic of Italy. The Lombards were succeeded, in turn, by the Normans, under whom Campania became a province of the kingdom they had established in Sicily. During the 12th century, under the Hohenstaufen dynasty, the region enjoyed renewed vitality, especially as a result of the growing importance of Naples. The capital of the kingdom was in fact removed to Napes when the Angevins succeeded to the throne of the Hohenstaufen. Their rule coincided with a cultural efflorescence (University of Naples, Medical School of Salerno) and with the expansion of trade; growing wealth was reflected in public and private buildings with which the region's towns were embellished. In the mid-15th century the Aragonese came to rule in their stead; after only sixty years they were replaced by the Spanish viceroys. The period of Spanish domination was politically turbulent (e.g. Masaniello's revolt) but artistically splendid (Tasso, Giordano Bruno, Cimarosa, Paisiello, Pergolesi). In 1734 Bourbon rule over Campania began. Under Charles III, Naples and especially Caserta, as well as many other centres in the region, were enriched with

magnificent works of art; but the other sovereigns of the Bourbon dynasty were hardly inferior in their patronage of the arts.

The rule of the Bourbons ended in 1860 and, following the conquest of the Kingdom of the Two Sicilies by Garibaldi and his "Thousand", Southern Italy was absorbed by the Kingdom of Italy. Henceforth the destiny of the region was inextricably merged with that of the nation as a whole.

AN OVERALL VIEW

Campania covers an area of 13,500 square kilometres. It is occupied in large part by the Campanian Appennine range and the Cilento and Matese massifs. The region's morphology is also distinguished by a series of volcanic outcrops, such as those of Vesuvius and Roccamonfina, as well as the Phlegraean Fields and some of the principal islands in the Gulf of Naples. The coast of Campania extends for over 350 km; it is low and sandy, and also precipitous and rocky, while the coastline is indented with a series of large bays (the Gulfs of Naples, Salerno, Gaeta and Policastro). A long and very fertile coastal plain runs between the Appennines and the sea. The hydrography of Campania is above all determined by the Volturno, Garigliano and Sele rivers, but there are many other lesser watercourses, including the headwaters of several rivers flowing into the Adriatic. The region can also boast of a large number of thermal and mineral springs, some of them already famous in antiquity.

The economy of Campania is mixed. Agriculture, which was formerly the major resource of the region, is not uniformly distributed. The coastal plain has in fact always been favoured for farming, its fertility enhanced by more favourable climatic conditions, better irrigation and especially the enrichment of its soil by volcanic sediments. The area is mainly cultivated with fruit and vegetables, which are largely exported to the rest of Italy and abroad, and also provide the staple ingredients of a flourishing preserved food industry. The same conditions do not apply to the region's hilly and mountainous area, in which the various environmental factors do not permit any substantial development of agriculture; this, combined with other factors, has in the past determined high emigration towards America or the rest of the country.

As regards to industry, Campania has assumed a leading role among the regions of Southern Italy.

The main industrial centres in the region are the cities of Naples and Salerno (with heavy industry predominantly located in the Naples area). By far the most important sector is the food industry, especially canning and preserved foods.

Some importance of the region's economy in also attached to fishing and more particularly the maritime trade concentrated in the port of Naples, the second largest in Italy, even though it is far from achieving optimum capacity.

Handicrafts, too, still play an important role in the economy of Campania. They have a centuries-old tradition and continue to provide a livelihood to many families, women in particular, in each of the region's towns and villages. The various arts and crafts for which the region

is famous include ceramics (the Capodimonte wares being especially famous) and the working of coral (its major centre at Torre del Greco). Other handicrafts include woodcarving, wrought iron, wickerwork and embroidery. All this, combined with the inestimable treasures and impressive remains of the great civilizations of the past, have made Campania a region of great and varied attraction, and one that has won its way into the hearts of countless people all over the world.

Naples sea terminal and view of the bay with the mass of Vesuvius in the background.

Naples

Naples, capital of the Region, is deservedly one of the most famous cities in the world. Its appearance, its traditions, its culture, the character of its people, the beauty of its monuments, and the splendid gulf on which it lies, are all features that have concurred to give it unique image. The classic photograph of the city spread out along the shores of the great curving bay, framed by that by-now famous pinetree, and dominated, in the distance, by the magnificent cone of Vesuvius, has made its way round the world, together with its songs, so full of sentiment and rich in poetry. The very name of Naples conjures up sunshine, the serenades at Marechiaro, the puppet figure Pulcinella, the feast of St. Januarius, the street urchins and the costumed criers of wares. It also conjures up spaghetti, pizza, and that typically Neapolitan knack, the "arte di arrangiarsi" (the art of arranging things to one's own advantage, smoothing over difficulties and looking aut for oneself) and the ingenuity displayed by the Neapolitan people in devising forms of livelihood. But - on the other side of the coin it also conjures up forced emigration and the pain of departure. Today, much has changed from an economic point of view, even though serious problems endemic throughout Southern Italy remain. Over the last few decades, the city has been subject to a process of rapid and often uncontrolled expansion; it has became an often chaotic metropolis in its helter-skelter race towards progress and industrialization. It has been subject to the upheavals brought about by modernization, both at the social and cultural, and at the economic and town-planning levels, with all the manifold ills effectina them. But its fate, from this point of view, is hardly different from that of countless other modern cities. Naples, which is today the biggest city in Southern Italy and the third biggest in Italy as a whole in terms of population, has Greek origins (it was called Neapolis, which means new city) and was perhaps initially a colony of Cumae or the Chalcidians. It quickly achieved considerable importance and prosperity. In the year 328 B. C. it fell under Roman domination, and throughout the long period in which it formed part of the territory of Rome, Naples maintained a position of great prestige: Roman patricians and writers loved to visit it and to build their villas in its beautiful environs, not merely due to their beauty and the agreeableness of their climate, but also to enable them to study and assimilate Greek culture of which the city had remained the greatest representative in Italy of that time.

During the medieval period Naples, protected by its walls and resisting various barbarian incursions, progressively reinforced all those mercantile advantages connected with sea trade which rapidly came to distinguish it from all the other cities on the coast and to turn it into an increasingly important trading centre. When in the mid-13th century the Angevins supplanted the Hohenstaufen, they chose Naples as the capital of their kingdom in place of Palermo; the city grew further as a result and the port attracted increasing numbers of merchants, capitalists, entrepreneurs and traders from as far afield as Pisa, Genoa, Florence and Marseilles. The fall of the Angevin dynasty was followed, in the 15th century, by the beginnings of the rule of the Aragonese under whom Naples extended its walls and expanded its importance as a trading centre. The Spaniards reigned over the city from 1500 to the early years of the 18th century: yet another foreign domination and yet again the need to adapt to a different system of government.

But Naples, especially under the Viceroy Don Pedro de Alvarez de Toledo, continued to expand (especially in the direction of the Vomero) and was remodelled by an ambitious building programme; one of the city's main streets is, in fact, dedicated to him (even though it has now been renamed Via Roma), while the baroque district to the west of Naples is also named after him. In 1734 the kingdom of the Bourbons began and it is to them that the city owes not only an improvement in its environmental

The magnificent Angevin Fortress, one of the major monuments of the city, was the residence of the rulers of Naples, and many famous personalities have stayed there over the centuries.
In the small photo: Triumphal Arch, the grandiose entrance into the fortress.

conditions, but also its embellishment with some of its most characteristic monuments: the Royal Palace of Capodimonte, the San Carlo Opera House, and many villas and Academies. The Bourbons continued to rule over Naples until 1860, when Naples and the whole of Southern Italy (the Kingdom of the Two Sicilies) - following Garibaldi's historic campaign - were finally annexed to the Kingdom of Italy. The 20th century has witnessed considerable demographic and economic growth in Naples.

This has been accompanied by a largely uncontrolled building boom, with the result that some beautiful hills and scenic spots like the Vomero and Posillipo have been engulfed by new buildings. In spite of all the problems and social ills that have accumulated over the years, Naples is making considerable efforts to put its urban and economic development on a more rational path and to implement a series of urban reclamation schemes aimed at halting inner-city decay and improving the urban environment.

THE CASTEL NUOVO – MASCHIO ANGIOINO

The Angevin castle known as the Castel Nuovo stands in the city centre of Naples, adjacent to the port which it dominates with its massive bulk and its series of beautiful cylindrical towers.

It was originally built by Charles I of Anjou, beginning in 1279, and served as the seat of the Angevin court. Under the Aragonese, in the mid-15th century, it was completely rebuilt by King Alfonso I and then assumed its appearance as a fortress in the true sense. At the same time it was embellished (among other things) with a Triumphal Arch entrance which constitutes a superb architectural and sculptural ensemble - indeed, one of the most important large-scale sculptural works of the 15th century. The two superimposed arches are richly decorated with narrative bas-reliefs celebrating the exploits of Alfonso.

Those who stayed in this splendid court included distinguished humanists and literati such as Lorenzo Valla and Panormita, and later Pontano, Caracciolo and Carafa.

Following the Carbonari riots in 1820-21, during the reign of the Bourbons, many patriots struggling for independence from foreign rule were imprisoned in the Castle.

Inside the Castle some interesting rooms may be visited, notably the Palatine Chapel, also known as the Church of Saint Barbara. It preserves in part its 14th century Gothic interior and its beautiful decoration. The Sala dei Baroni (today the seat of the municipal administration) in also impressive in size and in architectural structure.

Castel dell'Ovo: the massive fortress which rises out of the waters in the Bay of Naples was the original residence of the Angevins.

View of the façade of the Royal Palace. The building was designed in the 17th century by Domenico Fontana.

THE PALAZZO REALE

The Palazzo Reale, or royal palace, stands in the large and impressive Piazza del Plebiscito; facing it, on the opposite side of the square, is a semi-circular arcade dominated, at its centre, by the neoclassical Church of San Francesco di Paola. Magnificent and elegant in its scale and proportions, the Palazzo Reale was built in the early years of the 17th century designed by the architect Domenico Fontana. During subsequent years it underwent var-

ious restorations and transformations, the most important of which in 1734 and 1837 -this latter following a disastrous fire. During the 18th century, Luigi Vanvitelli (the architect of the royal palace at Caserta) also worked on the building; he was responsible for remodelling and harmonizing its façade.
The Palazzo Reale was first the official residence of the Spanish Viceroys, then of the Bourbons, and then, following the unification of Italy, intermittently of the House of Savoy. Today it is possible to visit the Royal Apartments, which house a fine collection of furnishings, ta-

pestries, porcelain and paintings. The Grand Staircase leading up to the Royal Apartments is particularly sumptuous, and the Royal Chapel is also of some interest. Adjacent to the Apartments is the charming Court Theatre. The Palazzo Reale now houses the Biblioteca Nazionale, one of Italy's most important national libraries; its vast holdings include printed books (divided into various sections), manuscripts, rare incunables and some valuable papyri discovered during the excavations of Herculaneum (in a villa which took the name of the Villa of the Papiri after the find).

THE SAN CARLO OPERA HOUSE

The San Carlo Opera House is located on the busy Via Vittorio Emanuele III in the centre of Naples. This theatre, famous throughout the world, was originally built by Charles III in 1737. It was subsequently enlarged and embellished by the architects Bibiena and Fuga. It was rebuilt by Niccolini in 1816, following a fire which had gutted its interior. The theatre enjoys perfect acoustics. Sumptuously and elegantly decorated, its six tiers of boxes provide seating for some 3000 spectators. It is principally used for the performance of operas, which continue to maintain a high artistic standard. The San Carlo Opera House can, indeed, boast a long and distinguished tradition in this field: the premieres of such famous operas as Doninzetti's Lucia di Lammermoor and Bellini's La Sonnambula were given here.

Left: *inside the Royal Palace, the splendid Throne Room.*
Below: *San Carlo Theatre (18th century), one of the most prestigious theatres in the world.*

THE GALLERIA "UMBERTO I°"

Facing the San Carlo Opera House, this impressive glass-domed gallery connects Via Roma, Via Vittorio Emanuele III, Via Santa Brigida and Via Verdi. It was built in a Latin-cross plan in 1887-90 and richly adorned inside with sculptures, stucco and gilding.

In the centre of Piazza del Gesù Nuovo; stands the spectacular and festive monument to the Virgin Mary, known as **The Guglia dell'Immacolata** - Dating to the mid-18th century, the monument consists of a baroque pinnacle adorned with friezes, volutes and numerous statues and on the top stands a statue of the Madonna.

PIAZZA DEL PLEBISCITO AND CHURCH OF SAN FRANCESCO DI PAOLA

This spectacular and harmonious square, with its semi-circular shape, was built in the 18th century. A long and elegant Doric arcade was added in the early 19th century by the will of the viceroy of Naples, Gioacchino Murat.

The Church of San Francesco di Paola stands in the centre; it is a building in the neo-classical style, and was constructed in the first half of the 19th century.

Above and right: Views of the entrance to the "Umberto I" Gallery and its splendid interior.
The gallery is an elegant and refined meeting-place for the people of Naples.
Below: Piazza del Plebiscito and Church of San Francesco di Paola.

THE CHURCH OF THE GESÙ NUOVO

In the same square is an interesting building dating to the late 16th century. It was built over the former Palazzo Sanseverino and retains part of its rusticated façade. The interior was built following a Greek-cross plan.

THE CHURCH OF SAN DOMENICO MAGGIORE

The church's present appearance is the result of a series of restorations which culminated in the baroque period; little remains of the original 13th century construction in the Gothic style, other than the main entrance. The interior of the church is large, sumptuous and impressive. It preserves the beautiful Gothic arches which divide the nave from the side aisles and which constitute the basic structure of the original building; the columns have, however, been sheathed in polished marble and the capitals gilded. The church contains a large number of admirable paintings and sculptures, including masterpieces by such famous artists as Caravaggio (his moving Scourging of Jesus) and Tino da Camaino (nine statues portraying the Virtues). The adjoining Convent once housed the famous University of Naples, particularly flourishing in the 15th and 16th centuries, which made the city a cultural and educational centre of the very first importance.

Church of Gesù Nuovo with its characteristic façade decorated with diamond-shaped rustication
Right: *inside the Church of San Domenico Maggiore.*

THE CATHEDRAL (CHURCH OF SAN GENNARO)

The Cathedral of Naples in perhaps better known as the Church of San Gennaro: after the patron saint of the city so dear to the hearts of the Neapolitan people, St. Januarius.

The church was built on the site of an ancient chapel towards the end of the 13th century. It underwent various alterations and restorations especially during the 15th century, but also during the 17th and 18th centuries, when it was remodelled in a baroque style and richly decorated in stucco. The principal façade, too, has undergone a number of alterations. The interior contains many interesting works both of painting and sculpture, and should be visited thoroughly. Many in fact are the artists who in the course of time have contributed to embellishing the church which houses the relics of the Saint so beloved by the Neapolitan people and so renowned throughout the world. Here we can only point out some of the chief works and especially the Chapel of St. Januarius, built at the beginning of the 17th century to honour the Saint who was believed, by his miraculous intercession, to have liberated Naples from an outbreak of plague. The Chapel, largely frescoed by Domenichino (notably the pendentives), preserves the relics of St. Januarius, particularly his blood. Among other note worthy works we may mention the Confession (or Carafa Chapel), situated in the crypt below the high altar and richly decorated in the renaissance style by Tommaso Malvito. The Minutolo Chapel, at the back of the transept, to the right, is the only one to retain its original Gothic structure and pictorial decoration. Adjoining the Cathedral on the left, and entered from a door in the left aisle, is the Chapel of Santa Restituta, which is an ancient chapel (4th century AD.) built beside the original church over which the Cathedral was built. At the end of the Chapel's right aisle we enter the Baptistery, dating to the 5th century AD.; it is particularly interesting, not only for its architectural features, but also for its often symbolic and particularly delicate decorations. According to tra-

dition, St. Januarius, bishop of Benevento, suffered martyrdom under Diocletian in the year 305 and was first buried in the catacombs of Naples (which today bear his name). During the transfer of his body to Naples, the Saint's blood liquified in the hands of the Bishop St. Severus, and ever since, this event has been repeated twice each year (in May and September). The remains of the patron saint of Naples were removed to the Cathedral in 1497.

THE CHURCH OF SANTA MARIA DONNAREGINA

The name in fact denominates two churches: at the back of the existing

Pictures of the interior of the Cathedral and the devotion of the people for St. Gennaro, the patron saint of the city. Left: façade of the Cathedral.

baroque church is in fact a far more interesting one of early 14th century origin. The latter is one of the most significant and artistically most valuable testimonies of medieval Naples and today, thanks to a painstaking restoration, it is possible to admire it in its original forms. On entering the church - after traversing a small but elegant cloister - we find, in the left aisle, the beautiful 14th century tomb of Queen Mary of Hungary, sculpted by Tino di Camaino and Gagliardo Primario. The chancel contains, apart from some beautiful choir stalls and a no less beautiful coffered ceiling, a cycle of important frescoes by Pietro Cavallini (14th century). The Apartment of the abbess in the adjoining convent also contains some fine works by Solimena, Mattia Preti and the school of Cavallini.

THE NATIONAL GALLERIES AND MUSEUM OF CAPODIMONTE

The National Museum of Capodimonte - a major collection of works of art - is housed in the former Royal Palace of the same name, built by Charles III of Bourbon in the early years of the 18th century. It is comprised of various sections, divided as follows:

a) The **National Gallery,** consisting of some 50 rooms in which are displayed a highly important series of paintings, in large part the legacy of the Farnese, Bourbon and Borgia collections. Many famous artists are represented: Simone Martini, Masolino da Panicale (The Assumption), Masaccio (Crucifixion), Botticelli (Madonna and Child with Angels), Pinturicchio, Filippino Lippi, Matteo di Giovanni, Colantonio, Sebastiano del Piombo, Correggio (among several works, the particularly beautiful Madonna and Child known as "La Zingarella"), Parmigianino, Giovanni Bellini, Vivarini, El Greco, Bassano, Titian (magnificent portrait of Paul III), and many Flemish painters.

b) The 19th Century Gallery, consisting of a suite of rooms in which neoclassical and other 19th century painters are displayed.

c) Of the valuable collection of the well-known porcelain of Capodimonte is displayed in various rooms, the Historic Apartment. Here we may admire, in particular, the famous salotto di Porcellana: a room entirely decorated in ceramics in the rococo style.

A visit to the richly wooded Park of Capodimonte is also well worthwhile.

The former gardens of the Royal Palace contain various ancillary buildings, including the former porcelain factory which achieved its greatest importance during the 18th century, the period in which it also produced its greatest masterpieces.

Royal Palace of Capodimonte, which houses the National Galleries and Museum of Capodimonte
Right: *inside the Royal Palace, the Reception Hall.*

Certosa di San Martino (St. Martin's Charterhouse) and National Museum of San Martino: view of the elegant cloister (above) and inside the church.

THE NATIONAL MUSEUM OF SAN MARTINO

The National Museum of San Martino was instituted in the mid-19th century in the Certosa of San Martino, a former Carthusian monastery founded by Charles of Anjou in the early years of the 14th century, but subsequently enlarged, enriched and rebuilt on several occasions. The Museum contains paintings, portraits, historical mementos, cartographic and topographic material, coins and medals, costumes and masks, and various other objects testifying to the history of the city of Naples, its culture, customs and folklore. The collection as a whole is a fascinating one, because it enables the visitor to gain a vivid and unique impression of many aspects of traditional life in Naples which are often ignored in history books, precisely because they belong to that sum of minor traits which nonetheless form an integral part of a civilization and its society. Also deserving particular attention is the Church annexed to the monastery. It contains important paintings by such masters as Guido Reni, Caracciolo, Ribera and others, and is also notable for its extensive intarsia decoration in marble. Adjoining the Church is the spacious Great Cloister designed by the 16th century architect Dosio and completed by Fanzago in the following century. Dosio was also responsible for the small cloister close to the church, a small masterpiece of Renaissance art.One of the elaborate Cribs displayed in the Museum of San Martino. It consists of over 700 separate pieces carved by the best known crib-makers of the day: a sophisticated handicraft with a long tradition in Naples. Many craftsmen were responsible for producing the varied and gaily-attired figures that throng the scene of the manger at Bethlehem: shepherds, blacksmiths, millers, carpenters, hawkers and strolling musicians - all of them clearly distinguished by their own individual features and costumes, and all of them eager - with typical Neapolitan warmth and generosity - to worship the Infant Jesus in his crib.

THE NATIONAL ARCHAEOLOGICAL MUSEUM

The National archaeological Museum in Naples is without doubt one of the major archaeological collections in the world, especially from a qualitative viewpoint, since its vast patrimony offers a uniquely comprehensive view of Greek and Roman civilization, especially as expressed in Southern Italy.

We owe the existence of the Museum, once again, to that prolific and distinguished patron of the arts and of learning, Charles III of Bourbon. In the building in which the Museum is now displayed - originally destined for the University of Naples - a variety of heterogeneous archaeological material coming from various collections, notably that amassed by the Farnese family, was gathered together and amplified with all the findings made during the excavations of Pompeii and Herculaneum, as well as other remains from Capua, Naples and Rome.

It is not possible here to give any comprehensive and detailed description of the innumerable works contained in the various sections, each with its own inestimable historical and artistic value. It should be emphasized, however, that the Museum offers an exceptional panoramic view of everything concerning archaeology of the ancient world.

To give some idea of its importance, we will cite just a few of the masterpieces it contains: the marble sculptures displayed on the ground floor, including the famous group known as the Farnese Bull, the Doryphoros and the Venus Callipygus; the valuable collections of prehistoric and Egyptian material; the collections of ancient bronzes, notably the beautiful Dancing Faun and the Drunken Silenus; the collection of paintings from Pompeii and in particular from the Temple of Isis; the several rooms housing mosaics, of which the large mosaic of the Battle between Alexander and

National Archaeological Museum; prestigious collection of classical art and of material and records from the archaeological sites of the Campania Region.

Darius, in the grandeur of its figural complexity and movement, takes pride of place; and the further suite of rooms displaying gold and silver objects, cameos and gems, and coins. We may further mention the marvellous series of still-life paintings that come from Pompeii, and represent not only great works of art in their own right, but a significant stage in the history of painting as a whole.

The Museum also contains a section devoted to the technology of antiquity which is of considerable interest, because it reveals aspects of ancient history and custom unattested in the art of that period.

National Archaeological Museum.
Above: *fresco depicting the Marriage of Venus and Mars (from Pompeii, House of Marco Lucrezio).*
Below: *the Farnese Bull (from Rome, Caracalla Baths) and statue of Caligula.*
Right: *fresco portraying Spring (from Pompeii).*

Capri

The island of Capri is one of the most precious gems of the Tyrrhenian Sea and the Gulf of Naples. A celebrated and much-frequented tourist resort, it already had the reputation of a holiday retreat in antiquity, as is testified by the remains of imperial villas (the striking Villa Jovis built by emperor Tiberius).

The island, easily reachable by ferry or hydrofoil from various points along the coast, consists of a series of rocky limestone hills, rising to the peak of Monte Solaro (589 m.), and a few small plateaux wedged between the escarpments. The coast is jagged and precipitous: the cliffs, and dramatic offshore rock outcrops like the famous Faraglioni, often rise sheer out of the azure water of the bay.

Capri is a miniature paradise. It is full of enchanting spots and an inexhaustible source of fascination, whether from the luxuriance of its vegetation, the beauty of its shoreline, with its everchanging waters, or the inimitable appeal of its strange rock formations and caves so magically illuminated by the reflections of water and light. Nature has truly lavished all her beauties here.

Capri is also the name of the main town on the island, which also comprises the smaller town of Anacapri and other villages.

A visit to Capri, which requires at least one whole day, must include the following various sights: first and foremost the picturesque and bustling town of Capri itself, the famous Blue Grotto, the Faraglioni, Anacapri (with its famous Villa San Michele), the Certosa di San Giacomo, the Villa Jovis, the Park of Augustus (public gardens), just to mention some of the main sights.

Capri: panoramic view of Marina Grande.
Following pages: *the magic charm of the Blue Grotto.*

PIAZZA "UMBERTO I"

This charming little piazza constitutes the fashionable centre of Capri: it's a kind of open-air drawing-room, elegant and flashing with colour. The piazza is dominated by the Torre dell'Orologio and the side of the Church of Santo Stefano. Al around it lies the characteristic medieval quarter of the town, which is substantially intact in its original structure, but diversified with innumerable shops, hotels and restaurants.

THE BLUE GROTTO

The reflections of light and shade, colours changing from azure to turquoise, from emerald to ultramarine, gleams of light refracted on the rippling water and on the rocky walls of the cave. Even sounds seem to take on th same unearthly hue as the sea, and th oars of the row boat which takes us int this fantastic, and yet utterly natura world seem to echo the beating of ou heart. We look around us to captur new sensations and to impress thi phantasmagoria of vivid colour in ou hearts. The light filtering through th entrance to the cave tells us that a rea world exists outside. But here, bathe in this otherworldly light, we give ou

*Capri: the central, picturesque square - piazza **Umberto I**.*

Capri: panoramic view of the coast of Capri.

selves up, for a moment, to an azure dream, just as the whole cave is azure. Now that the dream is over, now that we have reemerged from the Blue Grotto into broad daylight, let us speak of it in a rather more downtoearth fashion. It is basically a limestone cave hollowed out by the action of the waves. Already known in antiquity, it has always been admired for its beauty. The light that illuminates it and that gives the water its peculiarly radiant blue coloration, comes from an opening below sea level (its actual position has been determined by phenomena of negative bradyseism). Another small entrance to the cave above sea level permits access to small boats, but only with some difficulty, especially if the sea is not calm.

The visit to the cave is limited to its large central cavity. Yet in fact the cave continues to the rear, divided into several arms, before converging on a single point known as the Galleria dei Pilastri.

A short distance beyond this point Roman remains have been found. Others have come to light outside the cave, above the rock spur concealing its entrance. These remains recall to our minds the fact that Tiberius built a villa here, and testify to the reputation enjoyed by the Blue Grotto in Roman times. Its fame, indeed, must have been considerable even at that time, and although it is true that the cave seems to have been forgotten in the middle ages, its rediscovery (by the poet August Kopisch in 1826) was greeted with tremendous enthusiasm which added immeasurably to the fame of Capri in modern times.

The Blue Grotto is by far one of the most fascinating natural spectacles in the world: hence its great tourist appeal. What is a never-failing source of astonishment is the realization that its haunting beauty is produced by the unaided hand of nature.

Along the coast of the island are many more caves which, although less well-known than the Blue Grotto, are hardly its inferior in beauty and variety. We may mention the wonderful caves located in the vicinity of the so-called Arco Naturale (a natural archway in the rock): the White Grotto and the Marvellous Grotto in which the stalactites and stalagmites have created the most delicate and original shapes. Then there are the Red Grotto and the Green Grotto, the Grotto of the Saints, and those known as the Certosa, the Belvedere and the Arsenal. Only by circling the whole island by boat are we enabled to discover these - and many more - hidden beauties. The boat-trip round the island is indeed an unforgettable experience and permits us really to enjoy the variety of this coast, with its ever-changing succession of bays, promontories, rock walls, hidden coves, strange rock formations, and enchanting spots where nature still reigns supreme.

ANACAPRI

The other town of the island, Anacapri, is also of great charm. In position and urban structure it differs a great deal from Capri, and has its own unmistakable character. From Anacapri one can make excursions to Monte Solaro and the remains of Roman villas in the vicinity. Yet the most interesting visit in the town is that to the Villa San Michele, built by the writer Axel Munthe over Roman remains and on the site of a chapel dedicated to St. Michael, from whom the villa takes its name. Here, apart from admiring the villa's interior decoration and the antiquities found during the excavation conducted on the spot, we may enjoy the beautiful garden, from whence there is an incomparable panoramic view of the Bay of Naples.

THE FARAGLIONI

The strange and beautiful rock group known as the Faraglioni lies off Capri's Punta Tragara: another of the island's superb and inimitable natural features. The effect they create, heightened by the splendour and colour of the sea, is that of an enchanting and fabulous landscape.

The Faraglioni consist of three rock outcrops which rise precipitously out of the sea to a considerable height. They are separated from the mainland by a narrow strait. Roman remains have been found on the rocks, but now they are given over to seagulls.

View of Anacapri: *the other village on the island of Capri*
Rigth: *the Faraglioni, the splendid rocks which emerge from the sea of Capri.*

Ischia

The island of Ischia is the largest of those situated in the Gulf of Naples; together with Procida and one or two still smaller islands, which encloses its northern approach.

Its fame and beauty have long rivalled those of Capri and even in antiquity Roman emperors chose it as a resort.

The island is in fact one on which nature has lavished its finest gifts: a genial climate, picturesque spots, luxurious vegetation, enchanting panoramas, charming villages - today equipped with the most up-to-date tourist facilities - and a coastline notable for the transparency and brilliance of its sea.

The island of Ischia, which is volcanic in origin, is also endowed with another resource: its mineral waters and thermal springs. They are numerous and have been known since antiquity: in fact, many illustrious Romans came here to take advantage of the water. The springs have now been suitably organized by the construction of thermal establishments for therapeutic purposes.

The island of Ischia comprises six small municipalities: Ischia itself (the capital and most important centre), Barano, Casamicciola, Forio, Lacco Ameno and Serrara Fontana.

THE ARAGONESE CASTLE

The town of Ischia consists of two parts: Ischia Ponte, which is the older part, mainly inhabited by local fishermen and characterized by its small houses built out of tufa and other volcanic stone which gives it its peculiar coloration, and Ischia Nuova, the new town, which has been extensively developed as a modern tourist centre and a major seaside and thermal resort.

In the old part of Ischia, a stone causeway (the Ponte Aragonese) leads across to the tiny island on which the Castle is built. It was on this island that the inhabitants of Ischia sought refuge when a volcanic eruption destroyed the town in 1301.

The Castle is in fact an amalgam of various buildings attributable to different periods, since the people of Ischia continued to inhabit it till the 16th century. The causeway joining the island to the mainland was built by Alfonso of Aragon in 1478.

Picturesque view of Ischia Porto and the harbour.

Above: *the Aragonese Castle on Ischia.*
Below: *the picturesque centre of Ischia Ponte, the oldest part of the town.*

CASAMICCIOLA TERME

The little town of Casamicciola is situated a few kilometres west of Ischia on the island's northern coast.

Rich in mineral water, it has become a famous and much frequented thermal resort. The major tourist and bathing facilities are concentrated in the lower part of the town. The upper part, laid out along the slopes of the green hill to its rear, forms a quiet and agreeable residential area.

LACCO AMENO

Lacco Ameno is one of the best known and most frequented places on the island. It is famous for the minuscule island known as the "Fungo" (mushroom) which has assumed its peculiar shape as a result of the millennial process of water erosion.

Lacco Ameno lies on a secluded and picturesque bay, and a series of other small bays diversify its neighbouring coastline.

At Lacco Ameno, too, there are numerous thermal springs which are extensively used for therapeutic purposes. The island's volcanic properties are also envinced by some fumaroles - vents in the ground from which steam is emitted - situated on the outskirts of the town.

Above: Casamicciola - view of the coast and beach facilities.
Below: Panoramic view of Lacco Ameno and its characteristic "mushroom".

FORIO

The town of Forio lies on the western coast of the island. It is dominated by mount Epomeo, the highest peak on Ischia; its lower slopes are cultivated with vineyards which produce the well-known wine named after the island.

Forio, a charming and popular seaside resort, suffered, in the past, more than the other settlements of Ischia, from the incursions of pirates. This is the reason for the many watch towers built all along the coast The most massive and conspicuous of these is the Torrione, a 15th century bastion within the town itself which was transformed, once its defensive role had been superseded, into a prison and then into a museum.

The sanctuary known as the Santuario del Soccorso, full of the ex votos of seamen, is situated on the promontory of Forio, overlooking the sea.

SANT'ANGELO

Sant'Angelo is a small fisherman's village which has recently been developed into a seaside and thermal resort. It is situated on the southern coast of the island, close to the promontory of Sant'Angelo, joined to the island by a narrow isthmus.

Proceeding east from Sant'Angelo, we come to the long and beautiful beach of Maronti, a narrow coastal strip hemmed in by high cliffs. A number of powerful fumeroles and hotwater springs, some of them used for therapeutic purposes, are to be found along the shoreline.

The coast here is indeed of great fascination; the landscapes are varied, and the panorama is beautiful and extensive.

Above: *Forio the beach.*
Below: *Sant'Angelo: panoramic view.*

Procida

Procida is a small island of volcanic origin situated between the Cape of Misenum (delimiting the Gulf of Naples to the north) and Ischia. The island consists of pumicestone and tufa and its volcanic origins - like those of the nearby Phlegraean Fields - are also testimony to ancient craters.

Procida has a highly diversified coastline, and the tour of the island by boat is thus of considerable interest, enabling us as it does to admire both the variety of its landscape and the beauty and limpidity of the sea along its coast.

Procida is also the name of the only town on the island: situated on the north coast, it is of great charm for its flatroofed, differently coloured houses, with their orientalizing air, its silent alleyways wedged between the houses and passages underneath arches large and small, and its little stairways climbing the steep slopes on which the town is built. Procida is especially delightful, however, because it has somehow maintained intact its character as a simple little community of fishermen and farmers. One has only to look around: fishing nets lie in rolls along the beach and before every door; fishing boats rest on the sand. The tour of the island by road is also of great interest and offers a series of magnificent panoramic views. Especially beautiful are the two bays of Corricella and Chiaiolella, the latter occupying the crater of an ancient volcano.

Above the town, situated on a precipitous rock overlooking the sea, are the massive walls of the Castle, which now houses a prison.

Procida: view of the town.

Pompeii

Pompeii was founded by Oscan people in the 8th century B.C. It then fell under Greek domination, in view of its favourable situation close to the sea. The Greeks were ousted, in turn, in the 5th century B.C., by the Samnites, who ruled over it until Rome's growing expansion southwards eventually absorbed Pompeii into its orbit Pompeii then became Roman and was transformed into a city splendid for its monuments, prosperous in trade, and of great social and cultural importance. But its fortune and splendour were of short duration: its end was already near. Already in 62 AD. a violent earthquake had gravely damaged its buildings and decelerated its economic life. Hardly had its buildings been restored and its commercial activity revived when a new cataclysm sealed Pompeii's fate for good. On 24 August A C. a sudden eruption of Vesuvius buried the town beneath a pall of ashes and dust. Many of the citizens of Pompeii succeeded in escaping in time, but many others were engulfed in their homes or suffocated to death as they attempted to flee through the streets of the town.

The tragic end of Pompeii signalled the beginning of its modern history. The very fact that it was struck by a mixture of volcanic ash and dust meant that is was not destroyed, but only buried. This is a factor of the greatest importance, since it has enabled the Roman city to be recovered almost intact and has also facilitated the task of excavation, in view of the lightness of the volcanic detritus covering the site.

The excavations began casually and for a long time were pursued without scientific rigour or due organization. It was only in the 19th century, thanks to the archaeologist Fiorelli, that the ruins began to be systematically explored and carefully preserved; these controlled excavations, conducted according to scientific criteria, enabled over half of Pompeii to be brought to light. We are thus able to-

Overall view of Vesuvius and the archaeological site of Pompeii.

day to gain a comprehensive and detailed picture of a Roman city of essentially commercial character and to visualise it in its most disparate aspects: its everyday life and customs, its art, its, furnishings, its building techniques and the processes used in its trades.

Our knowledge of Pompeii is also important for enabling us to understand the developments of Roman architecture and more especially the transformations of its houses. We find in fact the most ancient and most simple type of Roman house, consisting of a massive construction enclosed on the outside and a group of rooms inside arranged round a central atrium, with a roof sloping inwards towards the centre for the collection of rainwater and a garden to the back of the house. From the 2nd century B. C. onwards the typical Pompeian house tended to become larger, more patrician in style and more lavish in decoration by the inclusion of a peristyle, a flower garden and new and more spacious rooms.

No less important is the opportunity of following the main developments of Campanian painting, which is well represented at Pompeii. Four main styles can be identified: firstly, a type of painting in incrustation style (1st century B.C.), consisting of simple rectangles in bright colour, in imitation of mar

ble, and framed with stucco; secondly, the perspective style (second half of 1st century B. C.), based on framing landscapes or perspective friezes with illusionistically receding architectural screens or columns; thirdly, the so-called "real

wall" style (1st century AD.) devoid of architectural illusionism, the wall surface being divided into brilliant monochrome panels; and fourthly, the illusionistic style, in which the plane of the wall is again illusionistically dissolved into landscape and architectural vistas and decorated with delicate ornamental friezes.

Lastly, Pompeii is important for reconstructing the various types of workshops, the development of public baths, hostels and other typical urban facilities. At Pompeii in fact we are able to recognise a complete city,

Pompeii: view of the central Forum and the remains of the buildings which once stood there.

with its Forum, its temples, its theatres and amphitheatres, its commercial area and popular quarters, its shops and taverns.

Anyone who tours Pompeii is able to see its bars and wash-houses, its wheat-mills and bakeries, its central heating systems, its gambling dens and brothels. He will find its walls still scrawled with electioneering propaganda, announcements of public entertainment, shop signs and, in the

rooms of cheap little lodging houses at the edge of the town, the joking graffiti of customers who stayed there for the night.

These excavations, therefore, offer us a good deal more than the usual archeological remains; they are the still-living testimony of the everyday life that went on in a Romanized town two millennia ago. More particularly, they offer a complete picture of its social conditions, customs and prac-

tices; they enable us **a** glimpse of the sumptuous villas of the nobility or the rich mercantile bourgeoisie and the poky little rooms of the servants, the slaves and the less well-to-do; the stores of great merchants and the cramped premises of small shop-keepers. In this way, ancient civilization as a whole gains a new immediacy, a new vividness, a new value, because it enables us to grasp the more tangible, human and down-to-earth aspects of life, which are often so similar to those of our own day that we seem to be seeing moments of daily life captured for all time.

THE FORUM

Pompeii's Forum is a large open space, elongated in shape and enclosed by a colonnade. With its surrounding public buildings, it constituted the city's political, religious and economic centre. Apart from the Temple of Apollo, these buildings included the Basilica, the Temples of Jupiter and Vespasian, the Building of Eumachia and the Macellum (or hall for the sale of provisions). The Forum was also the site of the Comitium for the election of magistrates, the pub-

lic treasury, and a series of stores serving either as warehouses or shops for the sale of various merchandise. Religious ceremonies, public declamations, slave trade and the daily market all took place in the Forum.

THE BASILICA

The Basilica, facing the Temple of Apollo on the Via Marina, was undoubtedly the largest and most imposing building in the city. It was used both as law-courts and a market. Consisting of a nave and two aisles

Pompeii

Above: *Porta Marina, the main entrance to the excavations of Pompeii.*
Below: *Remains of the Basilica in the Forum.*

separated by columns (not by chance were Christian basilicas modelled on the plan of Roman buildings of this type), the Basilica is preceded by a portico and ends in an elevated tribunal, of seat for the presiding magistrate.

TEMPLE OF APOLLO

We enter the excavations of Pompeii through the Porta Marina which is not the most important gate into the ancient city, but is the one providing the easiest access to the central area occupied by the Forum.

The Temple of Apollo is situated in this area, one of its sides abutting onto the elongated rectangular square delimiting the Forum. The Temple is peripteral and surrounded by an imposing arcade of 48 columns. The capitals are Corinthian, but part of the structure they supported was rebuilt and redecorated at a later period.

The Temple itself, raised on a high podium, stands in the centre of this court and is approached by fourteen steps, surrounded by a Corinthian colonnade,' and has a façade of six columns. It was preceded by a sacrificial area. The column to the left of the steps leading up to the Temple bore a sundial, accompanied by the dedicatory inscription of the consuls responsible for its installation.

The Temple of Apollo must have been not only one of the most important in the city, but also one with the most ancient origins, since an area sacred to Apollo, and thus some simple construction of which all trace has been lost, existed here already in Samnite times.

Placed against the columns of the Temple's portico are copies of the bronze statues of Apollo and Diana: the originals are now preserved in the National archeological Museum in Naples.

View of the Temple of Apollo.

Above: *the Forum, one of the memorial arches beside the Temple of Jupiter and the Macellum.*
Below: *building of Eumachia aerial view of the whole.*
Right: *Forum: Altar from Temple of Vespasian.*

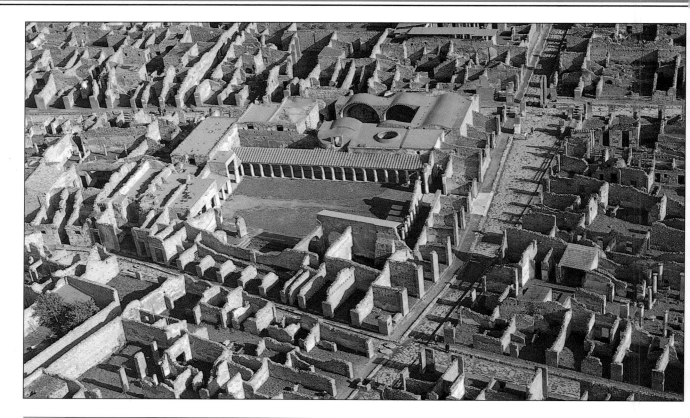

Above: *one of the bath complexes in Pompeii.*
Below: *Triangular Forum.*
Right: *Via dell'Abbondanza "Abundance Road", the main street in the town.*

HOUSE OF THE VETTII

The villa, one of the most beautiful and luxurious in Pompeii, takes its name from its owners, Aulus Vettius Restitutus and Aulus Vettius Conviva. The family belonged not to nobility, but to the rich merchant class.

In plan and structure, the villa is not very different from others of its kind, but what differentiates it from them is its magnificent pictorial decoration. Of particular interest is that of its sumptuous triclinium, whose walls are painted with a delicate frieze of cupids engaged in a variety of pursuits.

House of the Vettii; details of the frescoes belonging to the Cupids cycle.

THE VILLA OF THE MYSTERIES

This villa forms an architectural complex notable for the extensiveness and organization of its component parts. Built on the outskirts of the town, it is perhaps the most splendid example of the luxury and refinement of Pompeian villas, although signs of its later decline - it was damaged in an earthquake in 62 AD. - and transformation into a more modest country house are evident. Yet the Villa of the Mysteries is justly famous for its magnificent pictorial decorations; these are excellently preserved and of high artistic value. The paintings consist of the "cycle of the Mysteries" (from which the Villa takes its name): a frieze forming a continuous figural composition round the walls of a large room, and probably dating to the 1st century B.C..

THE CYCLE OF THE MYSTERIES

Although this cycle of paintings is still beset by many doubts about its interpretation, it seems fairly clear that we are dealing with the representation of the ceremony of initiation in the Dionysiac mysteries, which were widespread in Campania. The paintings, undoubtedly the work of a major Roman artist, belong to the first period of Campanian painting and constitute the largest pictorial figural composition bequeathed to us by antiquity. It consists of a series of separate narrative scenes, but the impression is of an uninterrupted succession of scenes, of a slow and gradual process in the neophyte's initiation. What is also striking in the representation is the artist's capacity for synthesis: his reduction of the narrative scheme to its essentials.

Villa of Mysteries: the splendid frescoes of the Mysteries cycle.

The Vesuvius

Vesuvius, the volcano of Naples, soars over the Gulf and dominates the landscape with its unmistakable conical shape: it has for centuries been inextricably linked to its history, and forms an inseparable part of its life and character. Other Italian and European volcanoes may exceed it in size, as in potency and number of eruptions, but Vesuvius is undoubtedly the most famous and the best known ever since antiquity. Its fame is, indeed, especially linked to its catastrophic eruption in the year 79 AD., when its massive outpourings of lava and terrifying rain of dense ash and red-hot stones submerged Pompeii, Herculaneum and Stabiae, ancient Roman towns whose excavated remains testify to their former greatness and the scale of the catastrophe which sealed their fate.

Only some fifty years before the eruption several Roman scholars had commented on the mountain's volcanic nature. Seneca, a distinguished writer of the time, spoke of the earthquake in 62 AD. as a premonitory sign of its impending reawakening. A graphic eyewitness account of the eruption in 79 has also come down to us in a famous letter to Tacitus by Pliny the Younger (whose uncle the Elder Pliny was himself a victim of the catastrophe). That eruption, the first of which we have historical confirmation, has been followed by many others in the course of centuries, some of them no less destructive. The mountain's volcanic activity has varied in kind: ranging from premonitory earthquakes to extensive lava flows and devastating emissions of ash and stones. Many of these eruptions have wiped out whole towns situated along the mountain's flanks and obliterated vast cultivated areas, specially vineyards which - thanks to the fertility of the soil - produce excellent wines. Periods of volcanic activity have, however, been followed by prolonged periods of quiescence. At the present time, Vesuvius in not active.

It is clear that during such a long period of volcanic activity, Vesuvius has undergone many transformations, which have radically altered its shape. Suffice it to say that successive eruptions have deposited their debris; new craters and crevices have opened; and the height and configuration of the main crater have varied according to the different effects of the eruptions. The appearance of Vesuvius today is hence the result of its successive eruptive phases and the sum of the debris accumulated over the centuries. What is commonly called Vesuvius is in fact an amalgam of two mountains: Monte Somma and Vesuvius proper. The two peaks are - if we look a little closer - easily distinguishable: the characteristic conical shape is actually bi-conical. The peak of Vesuvius proper rises above the large crater of Monte Somma and has probably done so ever since the eruption in 79 AD., which is presumed to have formed both it and the circular valley which separates the two volcanos (and is known by two distinct names: Atrio del Cavallo and Valle dell 'Inferno. A visit to Vesuvius is well worth-while and undoubtedly provides a fascinating experience. The "Circumvesuvian" railway, accessible roads, a cablecar and itineraries on foot to the edge of the crater, enable the visitor to see the volcano's characteristic structure at close hand and to share in the atmosphere - at once awe inspiring and surreal - created by the most secret forces of nature. Up there, standing at the edge of the gaping mouth of the huge crater (some 600 metres wide and 200 deep), in the midst of fumes and vapours disgorged from the pit, we seem to be at the gates of a landscape at once infernal and wonderful. Looking about us, we may also admire magnificent panoramic views of the Gulf of Naples and the plain of Campania below.

Monte Somma and the large cone of Vesuvius.

Herculaneum

Herculaneum is the other large Roman town which was totally destroyed by the eruption of Vesuvius in 79 AD. Situated on the slopes of the volcano like Pompeii, it too had been seriously damaged by the earthquake in 62 AD., before being totally overwhelmed and submerged below a huge mass of mud together with ashes and pumicestone 17 years later. Its fate, then, was not quite the some as Pompeii: in contrast to the latter which was struck by a deadly rain of ash and small stones which left its houses intact and facilitated subsequent excavation, Herculaneum was buried beneath a thick stratum of volcanic lava which solidified within a short space of time.

This was a decisive factor for the history of archeological exploration of the site. In fact, although the existence of a buried ancient city was known the solidification of the lava making it into a hard and rock like strata preclud'ed the identification of its exact position. It was only by chance, at the beginning of the 18th century, that the first important archeological finding was made on the site, and more precisely in the area of the Theatre. Since then a series of excavations have been instigated, with shafts and narrow passages laboriously hewn through the hard covering mass, thus gradually revealing the structures of various buildings and houses. In the following century, the exploration of the site was put on a more scientific route and a large part of ancient Herculaneum thus brought back to light. Another sizeable portion of the town however still lies buried beneath the modem town of Resina.

By these various' excavations a past which had been presumed lost for ever was thus gradually disinterred: a past rich in history and art, and as fascinating as that of Pompeii, though at the same time very different from it. In fact, what is most striking at Herculaneum is the intimate appearance of its buildings; the atmosphere of everyday life preserved intact in its houses and shops and vividly conveyed by its surviving details - furnishings, cooking utensils, tools working. Everything has (as it were) been eternalized and survives in all its immediacy and beauty today. This is essentially due to the peculiar conditions under which ancient Herculaneum was buried. The lava, flowing through all its streets and houses and solidifying, actually helped to support and preserve their structures.

At Herculaneum it is also possible to gain a comprehensive picture of the various types of residence, which are more highly differentiated than at Pompeii. We can in fact distinguish an area mainly occupied by patrician residences (Herculaneum, too, was a favourite holiday resort of wealthy Romans who built sumptuous villas here) and another characterized by the houses of the less well-to-do. It is also possible to see several two-storeyed houses - almost unique of their kind.

A visit to the excavations of Herculaneum is thus full of variety and interest: villas, baths, shops, streets - every facet of the ancient town is there for us to see. Although Herculaneum has only been excavated in part, it can be deduced from its structure and layout that, in Roman times, it must have been less than half as big as Pompeii and that, at the time of the eruption, its population must have been approximately 5,000. The town's economic and political centre, based on the Forum, is still largely submerged below the modern town of Resina.

THE DECUMANUS MAXIMUS

The ancient town of Herculaneum was probably of Greek origin (according to a tradition, it was founded by the mythical Hercules, from whom it derives its name).

It has a regular gridiron town plan, orthogonally divided into rectangular insulae by a series of cardines (streets running north to south) and decumani (east to west). The De-

Decumanus Maximus (Name of the main east-west street in a Roman town). House of the Cervi.

cumanus Maximus was a wide street, in fact the main street, probably leading to the Forum, i.e. the town's religious and political centre. It was flanked by many houses and shops, including the residences of the patriciate or the rich bourgeoisie - as testified by their spaciousness and refinement. The street was also lined, in part, with handsome porticos. The Decumanus Maximus was probably intended for pedestrians only, since no traces of the ruts of carriage wheels, generally left by carriages on Roman roads, have been found.

THE HOUSE OF THE RELIEF OF TELEPHUS

This is one of the most beautiful and interesting houses in Herculaneum both in terms of its architecture and the layout of its rooms (some of which face onto a broad terrace), and in terms of the refinement of its extensive marble decorations.
The house takes its name from a beautiful relief representing the myth of Telephus.

THE BATHS

Two thermal buildings have been found at Herculaneum: one larger and more complex, the other built at a later period and located in the suburban part of the town. Both are of considerable interest, however, for their architectural features, their heating systems and their decoration.
The main thermal complex - of which we see a detail in the accompanying plate - is situated in a more central location, and is divided into separate sections for men and women, as was usual in Roman baths. The various rooms (frigidarium, caldarium and tepidarium) are distributed round a central courtyard of Palaestra. Of particular interest is the mosaic flooring depicting marine animals.

The term Phlegraean Fields denominates an extensive area to the west of Naples which has from time immemorial been a scene of volcanic activity. The area comprises a territory stretching from Cumae (in the north) to Cape Misenum with its offshore islands of Ischia and Procida and the area to the south of Naples. In fact, apart from the major volcanoes of Vesuvius and Roccamonfina (now extinct), the whole of this tract of land was subject in prehistoric times, especially during the Quaternary period, to volcanic phenomena and as a result is dotted with craters. The very name "Phlegraean" is an indication of its remote geological origins: "flegraios" in Greek means "flaming lands" or "burning lands". It may be said indeed that the whole Campanian plain, as well as its offshore submarine platform and the islands lying off Cape Misenum, were formed by the accumulation and sedimentation of volcanic material, with the consequent morphological change undergone by the territory in the course of time. An intense and varied process which was protracted, in alternate phases, for several million years.

Today the Phlegraean Fields are still characterized by various phenomena of secondary volcanism: solfataras, thermal springs, mofettes, fumaroles and other volcanic vents in the ground. These are the objects of study by geological experts, as well as tourist attractions.

THE SOLFATARA

The Solfatara, the crater of a half-extinct volcano near Pozzuoli, has given its name to a phenomenon of secondary volcanism for which the crater is famous: namely, volcanic fissures emitting sulphurous gases, water vapour or hot mud. These phenomena are connected, more or less directly, to phenomena of volcanism proper, since they share the same endogenous origin with them. More precisely, they represent the last manifestations of a volcanic process on the way to extinction. The fissures known as solfataras emit vapour at very high temperatures; the vapour is mixed with carbon dioxide and other components including sulphur (from which in fact the crater derives its name). The Solfatara crater has a circumference of over 2 km., and also contains other phenomena of secondary volcanism, such as fumaroles (which are also exhalations of water vapour) and mofettes (emissions of carbon dioxide).

All these phenomena as a whole are of considerable interest. They also enable one to witness the condensation of water vapour, and thus the production of small clouds, if a source of heat that saturates them further is brought close to them: in fact, the volume of vapour is strikingly increased by holding a piece of burning paper in the stream of vapour rising from the fissures.

The Solfatara.

Pozzuoli

Pozzuoli is mainly visited as a seaside resort and as a spa and is of considerable interest both for its ancient monuments and volcanic properties. Of ancient origin (it was founded by Greek settlers in the 6th century B. C.), Pozzuoli - the ancient Puteoli - became an important Roman market town and commercial centre: the principal depot for trade with Egypt and the East. Signs of its ancient importance and prosperity are evident in its many surviving monuments, including the ancient Roman pier (the Moles Puteolanae) dating to the Augustan period and the Flavian Amphitheatre, built by the emperor Vespasian. The latter, one of the largest extant, began to be excavated at the beginning of the last century. The tiers of seats in the interior were divided into four compartments, while the imperial seat was distinguished by Corinthian columns of black marble. Of

Pozzuoli: view of the port area and the splendid coastline.

particular interest are the various subterranean structures below the arena, as revealed by excavation in 1838; they are very well-preserved and give us a very clear picture of the mechanics of holding gladiatorial games: the air-holes and outlets of the dens of the wild animals, and the conduit used for flooding the arena for the staging of naval combats, are all clearly visible. The most famous monument of all is, however, the Serapeum, a splendid building dating to the Flavian period and used as a market-hall. Apart from its intrinsic architectural importance, the fame of the Serapeum is especially linked to the volcanic phenomenon known as bradyseism which is particularly evident here. Bradyseism determines a slow raising and sinking of the ground. If we look at the columns of the Serapeum, we may note that they are covered with molluscs up to a height of 3 metres. This demonstrates that the building, initially erected close to the water, gradually sank below sea level and later rose again to its present position.

Aerial view of the Temple of Serapis.
Aerial view of the Amphitheatre.

The route leading from Pozzuoli past the Lake of Avernus to Baia, and then on to Bacoli and Cumae, is one of the most charming in the Phlegraean Fields: notable not only for the unusual beauty of its landscapes, but also for the splendour and variety of its ancient remains.
Ever since antiquity Baia was a much-loved bathing and thermal resort. In Roman times, it became a fashionable place of recreation for wealthy patricians, especially on account of its hot springs and abundant mineral waters, which were used for therapeutic purposes.

ARCHAEOLOGICAL PARK

The excavations carried out on the site have revealed substantial portions of the buildings which the bradyseismic phenomenon had buried.
The large and splendid baths have thus been brought back to light. They consist in fact of an ensemble of three buildings (the thermae respectively of Sosandra, Mercury and Venus); these date to different periods and are heterogeneous in style, yet are organically interconnected.
Close to the baths, in the vicinity of the pier, is the beautiful Temple of Venus; it has an octagonal plan and a circular interior.

THE CASTLE OF BAIA

The massive bulk of the castle dominates the sea below from the headland on which it stands. Built by the Aragonese over the remnins of a Roman villa - which may even have belonged to Julius Caesar - today it houses the Archaeological Museum of the Phlegraean Fields, in which the Roman and pre-Roman archaeological finds discovered during the excavations in the area are on display. A fine collection of plaster copies of famous statues accompanies the collection of sculptures, inscriptions and household objects.
A few kilometres beyond Baia lies Bacoli, another important archeological centre in the environs of Cape Misenum.
The imposing remains which can still be admired here (especially the large vaulted reservoirs known as the Cento Camerelle and the Piscina Mirabilis) once belonged to the ancient town of Bauli.

Panoramic view of the coast at Baia. Archaeological Park - detail.

Cumae was one of the most ancient Greek colonies in Italy; it was al most certainly founded by the Euboeans from Chalcis in the 8th century B C. Situated on a volcanic plateau in proximity to the sea, Cumae achieved great prosperity and importance in the period from 700 to 500 B.C. It was also an influential cultural and religious centre. Later, however, it declined and on being taken by the Romans in 38 B.C., was reduced to a town of little importance. Given its origins and the splendour it enjoyed at the height of its power, Cumae represents an archeological centre of great importance, testified by the various remains located on the former Acropolis and the ruins of various temples. Yet Cumae's fame is especially associated with the most famous Sanctuary of antiquity: the Grotto of the Cumaean Sibyl. The Sibyl, commemorated by Virgil in the Aenead, was one of the most respected and feared oracles of the ancient world. Pilgrims and devotees thronged from all over the Greco-Roman world went to this grotto, hollowed out of rock and located close to the Lake of Avernus, i.e. the gate to the Underworld, to ask for a prophecy about their future life.

The Temple of Apollo is situated on a brief detour of the Via Sacra which led from the Acropolis of Cumae to the Grotto of the Sibyl. Dating to the Greek period, only its podium and the stumps of columns remain.

**Above: Cumae: view of the fascinating and mysterious Sibyl's Cave.
Below:Christian Basilica with the font of the Baptisterium.**

Castellammare di Stabia

Castellammare di Stabia derives its name from its location at the foot of a castle dominating the sea, and from the ancient town of Stabiae whose site it occupies. It is situated on the southern curve of the Gulf of Naples and forms the connecting link between it and the Sorrentine peninsula. Castellammare has a lot to interest the tourist: above all its beautiful situation and landscape. Located on the slopes of a promontory, it commands wonderful views of the Gulf of Naples and Vesuvius. In the second place, it is well endowed with thermal and mineral springs, which have been much prized for their therapeutic properties ever since time immemorial. Castellammare, as a result, has become not only a popular seaside resort, but also a favourite spa and centre for thermal cures.

Thirdly, the town, which is a modern and busy industrial centre today, has another undoubted asset: the memories of its Roman past represented by the excavations of Stabiae. The first findings were casually made in the early years of the 18th century, but it is only in recent years that permission has been given for more systematic and scientific excavations. While it has to be admitted - not without regret - that much of the site's sculptural and pictorial material was looted in the past, the existing remains are nonetheless of considerable interest. Of particular value are a beautiful series of frescoes and sculptures now displayed in Castellammare's Antiquarium. The remains of the Villa of Ariadne and another Roman villa, both well structured and finely decorated, may also be admired in the archeological zone. Beyond Castellammare begins one of the most fascinating and beautiful tourist itineraries Italy has to offer: the Sorrentine Peninsula. Nor is it by chance that writers and painters have vied with each other in celebrating the incomparable beauties of this peninsula in art. The variety and magnificence of its everchanging scenery offer a unique spectacle: high cliffs dropping sheer to the sea, and opening out here and there into little anchorages and inlets, with villages set amid lush vegetation and overlooking the transparent sea. The road following the coast from Castellammare to Sorrento reveals, at every curve, new beauties and opens up a constant succession of incomparable views; at times it descends to charming little beaches, at times it climbs up to a high plateau overlooking the coast. The views on all sides are of inexhaustible variety, and the many villages situated along this stretch of the coast, picturesquely enfolded in woodland, seem to have been set there by the hand of an artist. The first town we come to is Vico Equense, situated on a rocky eminence overlooking the Gulf of Naples. It is a popular tourist resort. The main part of Vico Equense lies, overlooking the sea, on top of a tufa plateau some 100 metres high, but further on its houses descend to the coast, where the bathing resort of Marina di Equa is situated. On leaving Vico Equense and then Seiano, another popular summer resort, and on rounding Punta Scutolo, we are suddenly confronted by the majestic and unmistakable panorama of the coast in the proximity of Sorrento. This stretch of coast is known as Piano di Sorrento; it consists of a wide and luxuriant plain, sheltered by the surrounding mountains and descending precipitously to the sea by sheer cliffs. The view of this landscape is one of the most captivating in the whole Sorrentine Peninsula. Its incomparable beauty was not ignored by noble and wealthy Romans, nor by writers of every age who have hymned its praises in their works. The excellent wines produced here have long been appreciated, too.

Today, this stretch of coast remains unaltered in its beauty, an abiding masterpiece of nature. Several resorts are located in this extensive and lush plateau stretching as far as Sorrento. Among the main ones we may mention: Meta di Sorrento, situated just over 100 metres above sea level; charming and peaceful, it is a favourite holiday resort.

A few kilometres beyond Meta di Sorrento we come to another small town: Piano di Sorrento. This is followed in turn by the resort of Sant'Angelo, situated very near to beautiful Sorrento.

66 "Return to Sorrento", says a famous song that is known the world over, no less than "O Sole mio". And with it, the fame of this splendid resort - the ideal place for a holiday, thanks to its marvellous climate, its beautiful coast and its incomparable scenery - has spread throughout the world. Lying at the end of the Piano di Sorrento - that plain remarkable for its lush vegetation, its vineyards, orange groves and woodland - Sorrento is magnificently situated on top of a tufa rock plateau which drops sheer to the sea below. The town itself is the most important in the peninsula named after it.

Sorrento boasts of ancient origins: it was in fact a Greek colony. According to a legend - no less poetic than the land it celebrates - Sorrento was once inhabited by those mythical sirens who with their sweet singing bewitched passing sailors, including Ulysses himself. It later became a Roman town and, like Ischia and Capri, a favourite holiday resort, especially favoured by the wealthy Roman nobility for its delightful climate. Even today, Sorrento retains, in its centre, the outlines of its ancient chequerboard town-plan (the cardo is the present Via Tasso, the street dedicated to Sorrento's most famous son, the poet Torquato Tasso, while the decumanus is traced by the present Via Cesareo). The town extends on its precipitous rock terrace to the edge of the sea, while a series of steep streets and stairways lead down to the harbour and narrow beaches below. Of particular cultural interest is the Museo Correale di Terranova, a valuable collection of sculpture, paintings, furniture and other art objects dating to the 17th and 18th centuries. Also highly recommended are walks in the town from where it is possible to enjoy magnificent panoramic views, or excursions by boat, which enable one to discover the hidden beauties of this coast, including fascinating caves such as the famous Grotto of the Sirens.

Panoramic views of Sorrento and the Campania coast.

Positano

We are on the other side of the Sorrentine Peninsula, on the fabled coast of Amalfi, yet another splendid jewel of this Campanian coastline that has already offered the visitor so many incomparable beauties. Once again, nature has created a fantastic and utterly unique succession of enchanting landscapes which defy the power of language to describe. In fact, to speak of the deeplyscored limestone cliffs dropping precipitously to the sea, or the picturesque villages clinging to the hillside or sloping down to delightful little beaches, or to describe the colours of the sea and the sky and attempt to discriminate their infinite gradations, is vain: it cannot hope to arouse the sensations which only a visit to these places can inspire. Each spot is a world on its own, a fantastic world which dazzles the imagination and inspires unforgettable impressions. Positano is the first jewel of this coast It's a very popular resort, notable for its picturesque townscape, built on terraces on the hillside or clinging to the rocks. The town is intersected by a network of alleys and stairways, clinging to the mountain slope, running under arches, or descending precipitously and tortuously to the sea below. The architecture of the houses, too, is distinctive: their façades are graced with broad balconies and several buildings are roofed with domes. Notable among these is the majolica dome of the church of Santa Maria Assunta. Interesting walks can be made from Positano up to Sant'Angelo a Tre Pizzi, the main peak overlooking the town. From here superb views can be enjoyed over a magnificent and still uncontaminated landscape. Excellent hotels and bathing and sporting facilities make Positano one of the most popular and fashionable resorts on the Amalfi coast.

Views of the town of Positano and the breathtaking coastline.

The Emerald Grotto and the Conca dei Marini

Having crossed over the Furore Valley, the road to Amalfi continues to hug the coast - suspended, as it were, between the mountains and the sea. This stretch of coast, too, is sheer and rocky; the high plateau of Agerola drops steeply to the sea, creating huge, massive and spectacular rock walls.

Along this stretch of coast we also find a fascinating cave: the Emerald Grotto. Its name, which recalls the more famous Blue Grotto in Capri, is in itself suggestive of the colour and the play of light on its water. In fact, the cave, which can be entered by a long flight of steps, offers the spectacle of yet another miracle of nature: the rock, the sea, the stalactites and stalagmites, and the irridiscent reflection of light on water, all combine to create a fabulous atmosphere.

On leaving the Emerald Grotto, we round the promontory known as Capo Conca and arrive in another charming seaside resort: Conca dei Marini. The road then continues along the coast, until, on passing through Vettica, a village set amid vineyards and olive groves, we catch our first glimpse of beautiful Amalfi.

The Emerald Grotto, one of the most fascinating and magical natural caves on this coast.

On leaving Positano, the road, where possible, hugs the coast, its curves opening up a neverending succession of picturesque sights. The mountains behind descend to the sea, here with gently rolling slopes, there with precipitous cliffs or deep gorges. If we look out to sea, we may glimpse, in the distance, the beautiful island of Capri, with its unmistakable mountainous flank. Looking backwards along the coast we have just left, we may discover ever new and ever changing views. The houses are clustered together into small villages and cling to the limestone rock, as if they emerged from it and were made from the same material, almost as if they were a natural projection to it. The bare and rugged rocks are frequently diversified with splashes of green, especially lemon groves. Below, the sea is wonderfully transparent, its blue more intense than ever. A series of promontories and headlands diversify the coast and conceal little villages and secluded beaches from our sight.

Beyond the first headland - Capo Sottile - lies Praiano, a charming fisherman's village and a favourite seaside resort on the coast of Amalfi. Initially, its livelihood depended almost entirely on fishing, but the beauty of its situation and the pleasantness of its climate transformed it into a popular tourist resort.

Beyond Praiano the landscape once again changes abruptly: the tiny bay of the Marina di Praia, with its charming little fisherman's houses, gives way to the spectacularly rugged Furore Valley, a deep rocky gorge dropping precipitously to the sea. The view of these sheer cliffs, and of the waves breaking at their foot, is awe-inspiring.

Above: *view of the coastline near Conca dei Marini.*
Below: *view of the town of Praiano.*

The town of Amalfi, which gives its name to the whole coast on which it lies, is one of the most renowned tourist resorts in Campania and in Southern Italy as a whole.

The town, so distinctive in appearance and so picturesque in situation, clings to the rock outcrops of the Monti Lattari and is wedged tightly into the narrow Valle dei Mulini (a deep ravine). The sea laps at its foot, and in fact Amalfi's ancient waterfront now lies under the waves, since the sea level has risen and sunk the lower part of the town beneath it. The result was that it was forced to grow and develop in a restricted and intractable stretch of land; this is why the houses impinge so closely on each other and why the roads and steps are wedged, like corridors, so tightly between the buildings, using up as little space as possible. Every-thing seems to be miniaturized, and every corner, every alleyway, opens up picturesque vistas.

This unmistakable agglomeration of white, tightly-packed houses rising up the hillside is dominated by the beautiful Cathedral which stands superbly on top of a great flight of steps leading up from the main piazza of Amalfi. It reigns unchallenged over the town with its distinctive architecture and brilliant sequence of poly-chrome marbles.

Today Amalfi is one of the most popular seaside resorts on the Campanian coast, thanks to its mild and agreeable climate, its beautiful situation and surroundings, and its crystal-clear sea. Yet its popularity is also a measure of its well-developed and sophisticated tourist facilities which have helped to spread its fame throughout the world.

Amalfi can also boast of a distinguished past. It is in fact Italy's oldest maritime republic and was the first to rise to eminence. Its greatness dates to the 11th century, but its origins are still more remote. In fact Amalfi, according to some historians, was founded by the Romans in the 4th century AD. But it did not undergo any considerable development until it was annexed to the Byzantine Empire, under whose protection it came to enjoy growing liberty. Such were the premises for Amalfi's later rise to independence and prosperity. In the political field, it defeated the Saracens and Lombards who threatened its existence, and put an end to the internal squabbles that weakened its rule, while in the commercial field, its agile ships sailed ever further and opened new markets. Amalfi thus became a prosperous seafaring nation and an independent maritime republic whose prestige long remained uncontested. Amalfi then extended its jurisdiction over part of the surrounding Campanian territory. It assumed the prerogative of minting its own

Overall view of part of the Amalfi coastline and the town of Amalfi.

Amalfi

coins and having its own Constitution. Very important from this point of view were the so-called Tavole Amalfitane which codified the whole question of trade in the Mediterranean. The laws and regulations enshrined in this pioneering code of maritime law derived from a careful study of the needs and practices of seafaring and mercantile life. Initially, they had the function of protecting the Republic's own ships, but were subsequently extended to the whole Mediterranean basin and became a universally respected code of practice. In fact, the Republic of Amalfi had greatly extended commercial bases and, with a powerful fleet, had reached the gates of the Orient.

The Republic's independence and splendour lasted until 1137, the year in which Amalfi was sacked by the Pisans, but previously she suffered major defeats at the hands of Robert Guiscard and his son Roger. It then lost though not entirely commercial importance, independence and condition as an autonomous Republic. Among the illustrious sons of Amalfi we may recall Havio Gioia whom tradition claims as the inventor of the compass. Yet recent studies have ascertained not only that this 14th century navigator had probably not been born in Amalfi, but that this important instrument of navigation had already been invented. It may therefore be presumed that he perfected it and that, thanks to his efforts, the compass came thereafter to be widely used in navigation.

Amalfi: *view of the small harbour.*
Right: *characteristic views of the town of Amalfi and its coastline of great charm.*

THE CATHEDRAL

The Cathedral of Amalfi rises, in all its splendour and elegance, over the Piazza del Duomo, adjacent to the Piazza Flavio Gioia, the main square in the town. Its Arab and Norman style confers a distinctive appearance and particular fascination on its architecture. The Cathedral was built in the 9th century, but was reconstructed at the beginning of the 13th century and subsequently restored and remodelled on a number of occasions. The façade, which collapsed in the mid-19th century, has been totally rebuilt in a style in imitation of its original 13th century forms. Beautifully decorated in polychrome marbles, it is preceded by a broad portico, while its tympanum above is ornamented with a mosaic. The magnificent bronze doors forming the main entrance to the church were made in Byzantium in 1066 and are adorned with inlaid silver work. The interior more clearly reveals the signs of later restorations though it does preserve some structural features of the medieval basilica, as well as some interesting pieces of sculpture by Bernini and Domenico Fontana and the relics of St. Andrew, patron saint of Amalfi.

Adjacent to the church stands the beautiful campanile (bell tower), in Arab style, which preserves its original structure intact. The portico of the church also provides access to the very pretty cloister (the Chiostro del Paradiso). Dating to the 13th century, it consists of an unbroken succession of Arab arches supported by twinned columns, surrounding a peaceful garden. A luminous, serene and mystic atmosphere reigns in the cloister. Various pieces of Roman sculpture - including two sarcophagi - and remaining fragments from the old church are preserved round its walls.

Right: *Amalfi Cathedral and its beautiful polychrome façade made of different kinds of marble.*
Cathedral interior.

Atrani

After leaving Amalfi, the coastal road climbs up a short promontory, from which a marvellous view can be enjoyed, before reaching neighbouring Atrani.

The small town of Atrani is charmingly situated at the entrance to a ravine - the Valle del Dragone - close to the sea, and at the foot of steep rocky peaks which dominate the town and the picturesque bay below.

In the past, the history of Atrani has been inseparably linked with that of Amalfi. In the beautiful church of San Salvatore in the central piazza, the elections, followed by the investiture, of the Doges took place. This church, which boasts of ancient origins, has been completely remodelled inside, though it still preserves from its original construction some beautiful bronze doors dating to the 11th century; of Byzantine workmanship, they are similar to those in the Cathedral of Amalfi.

Another interesting church in the town is that of Santa Maria Maddalena. Dating to the 13th century, it is graced by a charming majolicatiled cupola, a fairly typical feature of architecture in Southern Italy. From the piazza in front of the church a beautiful panoramic view of the coast can be enjoyed.

On leaving Atrani, the road continues along the splendid coast of Amalfi in the direction of Minori, Maiori and other enchanting spots, while another no less scenic road leads inland and winds in steep hairpin bends up the rocky mountainside in the direction of Ravello.

Characteristic views of the town of Atrani and its coastline of great charm.
Opposite: *the magic of the sea below Ravello, one of the loveliest towns on the Amalfi coast.*

We leave the coast road just outside Atrani and diverge to the left along a road which climbs, in long windings, over a rock outcrop dominating the Valle del Dragone. A short drive brings us to one of the most enchanting and picturesque spots on this coast: Ravello. Its superb position, on rugged spurs dominating the Campanian shoreline, its natural and artistic beauties, its unique atmosphere compounded of silence and solitude, its lush gardens and fabulous panoramic views, make Ravello an unforgettable resort, an oasis of peace and tranquillity. The history of Ravello can be traced back to the 9th century. Later its destiny became intimitely linked with the maritime Republic of Amalfi, and the economic prosperity consequent on that connection must have been enviable. It is clearly testified by the numerous patrician residences that still embellish the town and confer on it an elegant and distinctive appearance. The wealthy merchants who inhabited them made them the outward expression of their opulence and splendour. A visit to Ravello is thus of considerable interest from an artistic and cultural viewpoint, as well as from that of its scenic position. In the buildings of the town the oriental style is predominant: it testifies to the frequent contacts between local merchants and the entrepots of the Near East, and gives to the whole town an exotic and original flavour. A number of buildings are well worth visiting: the characteristic little church of Santa Maria a Gradillo, the Romanesque Cathedral and the beautiful Palazzo Rufolo (with its lovely garden, courtyard and terrace commanding panoramic views. Concerts in honour of Wagner, who had a special fondness for Ravello, are given here). We should also mention the magnificent Villa Cimbrone from whose famous Belvedere one of the most spectacular views of the coast of Amalfi can be enjoyed. Nor should we forget the Palazzo Confalone, the church of San Giovanni del Toro, the Moorish fountain, the ruins of the Castle, and the many picturesque alleys that crisscross the town.

THE CATHEDRAL

The Cathedral stands in the main square of Ravello, the Piazza del Vescovado, which is situated almost at the highest point of the town. The provincial road leads into this square, as also does the panoramic road which has recently been built to provide easier access to Ravello and to enhance the scenic beauties of the area. Dedicated to St. Pantaleone, the Cathedral was originally built by bishop Papirio in the later 11th century, but has subsequently undergone considerable alterations - especially in the 18th century - which have altered its spirit, though leaving its underlying structure substantially intact. This is the case of the portico which preceded the church, forming a large atrium: of it only four columns remain, since the rest collapsed as the result of an earthquake. The Cathedral is flanked by a handsome bell-tower dating to the 14th century, and entered through magnificent bronze doors made by Barisanus of Trani in 1179: they are divided into 54 relief frames decorated with scenes of the Passion of Christ, and are considered a masterpiece of 12th century art. The interior, which preserves its original structure in part, is notable for its magnificent Pulpit dating to the 13th century. The work of Niccolò di Bartolomeo da Foggia is finely decorated with mosaics, and rests on elegant twisted columns supported by lions. The Pulpit represents a wonderful fusion of the classic, Byzantine and Saracenic styles. Opposite it stands a no less magnificent Ambo, also decorated with a mosaic representing Jonah being swallowed by a whale. The nave and transepts are decorated with paintings of some value, while the choir is adorned with a handsome episcopal throne and paschal candelabrum. The Chapel of San Pantaleone houses the reliquaries of the blood of the Saint to whom the Cathedral is dedicated.

Interior of Ravello Cathedral - the magnificent pulpit made by N. di Bartolomeo (XIII century).

Panoramic view of Ravello and the coastline nearby.
Villa Cimbrone: from the terraces of the Villa there is an unforgettable view.

Minori

Continuing our itinerary along the Coast of Amalfi, we go back down the road leading up to Ravello and resume the coast road leading from Atrani to Minori and Maiori. The route is, again, a scenic one, with marvellous views of a succession of little bays and of green slopes of the peninsula, dotted here and there with houses and little villages, descending to the blue waters of the Tyrrhenian sea.

Hidden in the bosom of a secluded and lovely bay, amid an idyllic landscape, lies Minori, the ancient "Regina Minor" of the Romans. Its white, variegated little houses lie strung out along the coast, emerging from the rocks, or adapted to the terraced hillsides behind and peeping out from orchards and orange and lemon groves.

A small but beautiful beach, equipped with suitable bathing facilities, has turned Minori into a very popular seaside resort and holiday centre.

Just before entering Minori, on the Strada Santa Lucia, we may visit the impressive remains of a Roman villa. Its beauty and considerable size as well as the presence of other Roman patrician villas in the area (not all of them excavated or even certainly identified), confirm the importance of Minori during the Roman Empire and suggest that this stretch of coast was, even then, much frequented as a holiday resort.

At Minori we may also visit the Basilica of Santa Trofimena, built in the year 1100.

Attractive view of the town of Minori, one of the prettiest corners on this coast.

The town of Maiori is situated immediately beyond the small promontory that separates it from Minori. It is situated on a narrow alluvial plain at the mouth of the Tramonti Valley. The town can boast of a long sandy beach, a rather unusual feature along the generally rocky and precipitous Coast of Amalfi, and is welle-quipped with efficient and modern tourist facilities. In fact, Maiori has become an excellent and widely-known holiday resort.

In spite of its long sandy beach, the town's appearance and picturesque surrounding lanscape, with its terraced lemon groves, is not dissimilar from those of many other resorts along this coast. Its ancient name was Regina Major. In medieval times, it formed an integral part of the maritime Republic of Amalfi, whose destiny it shared. It was well fortified with defensive towers and walls, the remains of which are still visible.

A visit to Maiori may include the church of Santa Maria a Mare, one of ancient foundation but whose original medieval structure has largely been obscured by later restorations. Also worth visiting is the church of Santa Maria delle Grazie; it too is of ancient origin, but was rebuilt after having been destroyed - like so many other buildings in the town - by the terrible floods in 1910. On the coast near Maiori are some interesting caves, whose shape and the coloration of whose water resemble the more famous Emerald Grotto near Praiano and the Blue Grotto in Capri.

View of Maiori and its long sandy beach.

Erchie

Leaving Maiori behind us we continue our itinerary along the final stretch of the Coast of Amalfi. A few kilometres beyond Maiori we may note an ancient Norman tower overlooking the sea. Then, a short distance beyond, again on the coast, are the picturesquely situated ruins of an ancient Benedictine monastery known as Santa Maria Olearia, built on natural rock; with valuable Byzantine frescoes preserved in the church.

As we proceed towards the southernmost point of Capo d'Orso, we may enjoy splendid panoramic views of the coast behind us before rounding the cape and being greeted with the sight of the Gulf of Salerno spread out before us.

On rounding Capo Tummolo a short distance further on, we arrive in Erchie, a pretty little village spread out along a lovely sandy beach. It is dominated by an imposing and massive tower (the Torre di Erchie) built on a low but precipitous rock promontory. With its simple but agreeable appearance, its beautiful shoreline sheltered by the mountains to its rear, its salubrious climate and its comfortable facilities, Erchie undoubtedly represents a restful and peaceful spot. It derives its origins from the ancient Benedictine Abbey of Santa Maria di Erchie situated close by.

Erchie: picturesque view of rocky promontory.

Salerno is one of the five provincial capitals of Campania and a busy industrial and commercial centre. Situated to the north of the gulf which takes its name, it lies spread out along a narrow coastal strip which only further to the south broadens out into the alluvial plain of the river Sele - long since drained and reclaimed for agriculture. The hills which rise steeply to the back of the town are the Monti Piacentini, whose lower slopes descend to the edge of the town. Salerno, whose name probably derives from its situation between the sea ("salum") and the river Irno, has very ancient origins, as attested by the discovery of a series of tombs dating to the 5th century B.C. It was successively Greek, Etruscan and Roman. After suffering the consequences of barbarian invasions, it fell under the rule of the Lombards, who included it in the Duchy of Benevento. Later Salerno seceded from Beneventan rule and became an autonomous city-state. Conquered by Robert Guiscard in the 11th century, it became a Norman fief. This was a positive period in the history of Salerno, whose political, economic, artistic and cultural prestige grew: it became capital of the Regno; the city was graced with the beautiful Cathedral; and it was during this period that the famous medical school of Salerno was developed. This was the most prestigious medical school of the time: it attempted to combine the medical knowledge of the West and the East, and thus earned the title of "Hippocratic school" (after the most celebrated Greek physician) which came to be extended to the city as a whole. During the 12th century the importance of Salerno was eclipsed by that of Naples. It successively fell under the domination of the Hohenstaufen, the Angevins, the Aragonese and the Bourbons, until it was eventually absorbed, in 1860, by the Kingdom of Italy and united its destiny with the rest of the country. Salerno is mainly a modern city today. A busy industrial town, it is progressively growing - gradually spreading further and further along the coast with a series of new and functional housing developments. Yet a fascinating ancient nucleus still remains at the heart of Salerno; it is characterized by a maze of little streets, an irregular town plan, and a warren of houses clinging to the hillside.

THE CATHEDRAL

The Cathedral is Salerno's most important building. Its construction dates to the happiest period in the history of the town, when it was conquered by the Normans and chosen as the capital of their kingdom. The Cathedral was in fact erected by Robert Guiscard in the second half of the 11th century, and consecrated in 1085. In the course of the centuries, it has undergone various alterations, but a recent restoration has revealed its original structure. The Cathedral is preceded by a great arcaded atrium (the famed medical school of Salerno probably stood to its right). Entering through beautiful Romanesque doors (the Porta dei Leoni), the atrium consists of a long series of arcades of Saracenic type, supported by antique columns and surmounted, along the sides, by elegant loggias. Roman and medieval sarcophagi stand under the arches along the walls. A tall and elegant bell-tower stands to one side of the façade. The Cathedral is entered through the central portal with valuable bronze doors made in Constantinople in the

Salerno: overall view of the city and harbour.

Salerno

Salerno: The Cathedral.

11th century. The interior is impressive, despite the fact that later alterations and decorations have masked its original appearance, such as the stucco pillars which cover the ancient columns. Features worth noting are the rising floor and the asymmetrical transepts. The Cathedral's interior is adorned with numerous works of painting and sculpture. In particular, we may note the two wonderful pulpits, delicately decorated with mosaic inlays, the beautiful paschal candlestick, and the screen that separates the nave from the choir. A series of fine medieval tombs are also noteworthy, including the tomb of Margaret of Durazzo at the end of the left aisle. Also of interest are the Chapel of the Crusades of Pope Gregory VII (who is buried here), in which soldiers departing for the Holy Land were blessed: the high altar with magnificent marble decoration; and the Crypt in which the relics of the Evangelist St. Matthew are preserved.

Paestum, once called Poseidonia (from Poseidon, the Greek god of the sea), was of very ancient origin. The area was inhabited even in prehistoric times by Italic peoples. Tombs, grave-goods and other remains, excavated in the surrounding countryside, testify to this period. But the town itself was founded in the 6th century B.C. by a group of Greek colonists from Sybaris, who chose to settle on the site due to the fertility of its soil, which promised flourishing agriculture, and its closeness to the sea, which favoured seaborne trade.

And in fact ancient Poseidonia rapidly assumed a position of considerable prestige in the economic field: it became a prosperous commercial centre and exerted political and cultural domination over the surrounding area. Unequivocal testimonies to Poseidonia's greatness under Greek rule shows its considerable urban development and the great religious and secular buildings that adorned it.

The town's name changed to Paestum when it fell into the hands of the Lucanians in the 4th century. Lucanian rule continued until the Romans turned their attention to southern Italy and began to expand their domination there: Paestum fell to them in 273 B. C. The town thus became Roman, and all the elements of Roman civilisation followed in turn, though an original residue of Greek culture did persist. Under the Romans, Paestum retained its importance, too and was embellished with temples, a Forum, Baths and a complex of major public buildings.

The decline and fall of the town can be attributed to historical and political causes, such as the fall of the Roman Empire, but also to environmental factors due to on the progressive silting up of the mouth of the small river on which it lies: this led to the reversion of the land to marsh - with its attendant malarial disease - and forced the inhabitants to withdraw to the hills to the back of the town. The barbarian invasions did the rest. Paestum was abandoned and became a ghost town. Its magnificent buildings alone remained, but they too were destined to share the fate of the town they had embellished. This was not only because they gradually lost their importance (the pagan temples having been stripped of all meaning by the Christianity which took root here at an early period), but more especially because they

Paestum: panoramic view of the Temple of Neptune and the Basilica.

were the victims of continuous devastation and spoliation. The building materials spoliated in successive waves went to adorn churches and buildings in other towns (thus, large quantities of marble and sculpture from Paestum were used for the building of the Cathedral in Salerno). Abandoned and destroyed by human cupidity, the very memory of Paestum was lost. All its wonderful buildings and temples, fallen into ruin, were gradually covered over by earth and undergrowth, from which only the upper parts of the taller buildings emerged - or those that had not already collapsed and lay in a confused heap of rubble with the other remains. The rediscovery and reclamation of Paestum dates back to the 18th century, initially thanks to the interest and encouragement of Charles of Bourbon, a famous patron of the arts. Since then, more systematic studies have uncovered an extensive archeological area of the greatest interest. The site of Paestum today - as revealed by the excavations - is demarcated by a circuit of stout walls with a circumference of some 5 *km*. These walls deserve careful examination both to ascertain their method of construction and to understand their defensive system, based on the thickness of the blocks of stone with which the wall is built and the numerous guard-towers along its perimeter. The town was spread out within this extensive circuit of walls. It was orthogonally divided into four quarters by the town's main streets: the cardo and the decumanus, and adorned, in its central area, with a series of splendid temples which will be described in more detail below.

THE BASILICA

Archaic Greek art, and notably the temple of Doric type, is widely represented at Paestum. The temple type in question is characterized by the simplicity and solidity of its structural elements, the stability and compactness of its plan, the beauty of its proportions, and the assurance with which it dominates the surrounding environment. The temple known as the Basilica at Paestum represents a typical example of this. It is in fact the oldest building in the town (dating to the 6th century B.C.), and impresses us by its weightiness, compactness and solidity, and by the unchallenged firmness and solemnity with which it adheres to the ground.

The mighty columns which surround the temple (18 along each of the longer sides and 6 upholding the architraves on each of the shorter sides) follow each other at a slow and measured pace. The sense of strength and compactness is reinforced by the plain Doric capitals typical of all buildings of the archaic period. The columns are noticeably tapered: they are far wider at the bottom, slightly bulging in the centre, and gradually reduced in diameter towards the top. This contributes to give a sense of greater airiness to the building and slightly reduces the tension created by disparities in the weight of the upper and lower parts of the temple.

The columns support a massive architrave formerly decorated with paintings and sculpture. Nothing remains of the pediment. The Basilica, of which the elevated cella, or sanctuary, inside, divided by a series of columns into two halves, and all the fifty columns of its exterior arcading have been preserved, is a peripteral temple (i.e. surrounded by columns on all four sides). It measures approximately 50 x25 metres.

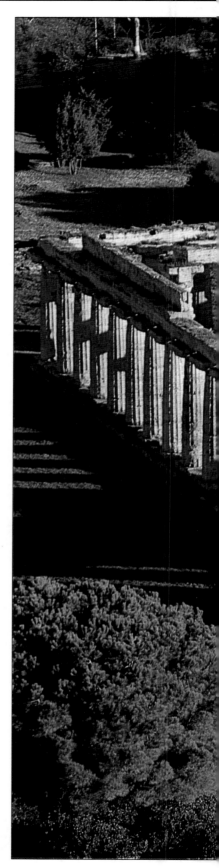

Paestum: Basilica.

THE TEMPLE OF NEPTUNE

Close to the Basilica stands the majestic and beautiful Temple of Poseidon (or Neptune), another distinguished example of Doric architecture. Although its general plan and individual components are similar to those of the temple we have just described, the spirit that animates it is profoundly different.

Built a century after the Basilica (around the year 450 B.C.), it shows that the art of architecture had attained a new maturity and that the forms previously expressed had also been perfected.

Although the building's archaic structure, its grandeur and strength, remain unchanged, we can sense a greater refinement in its structural components, which is also expressive of a different sensibility in the artist who designed it. This is especially apparent in the building stone used, which has assumed a mellow golden tone. This confers a different luminosity on the temple and renders the massive compactness of some of its structural elements, more evanescent and imperceptible such as the more flattened capitals and the columns, which are even more bulging in the centre, almost as if to render visible the greater weight they are supporting.

The Temple of Neptune is the best preserved of the temples at Paestum and one of the most beautiful that has come down to us from antiquity. It is peripteral - 14 columns along each of the sides and 6 at either end - and consists, internally, of a large cella divided into three aisles by two orders of columns. The temple was probably dedicated to the goddess Hera. The misleading names by which these temples are known today were conferred at the time of their rediscovery.

Aerial view

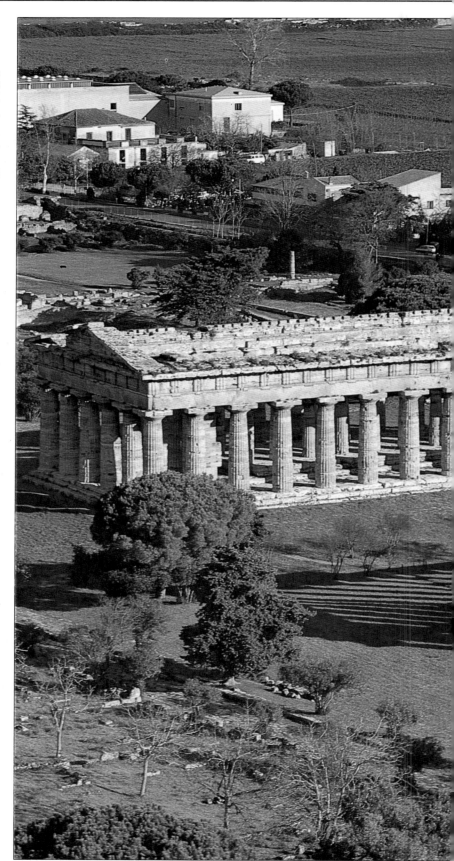

Paestum

Paestum: partial view of inside the Temple of Neptune.

THE TEMPLE OF CERES

The Temple of Ceres is on the opposite side of Paestum the Temple of Neptune and the Basilica, and constitutes, together with them, the most imposing preserved building of the ancient town. In structure, it is not very dissimilar from the other two temples: it too is a Greek temple of the archaic period, but chronologically is perhaps to be placed between the 550 B. C. of the Basilica and the 450 of the Temple of Neptune. Again we are dealing with a peripteral building, with six columns at each end and thirteen on each side. Its proportions are carefully worked out: in fact the sides are double the length of the front. The space occupied by the temple is thus more harmoniously disposed and aesthetically more elegant. The internal cella is elevated over a high podium; it is rectangular in shape and preceded by a colonnade of which only the lower parts remain.

In the Temple of Ceres we can also observe a greater degree of agility in the columns, although they reveal as usual a slight bulge towards the centre. The temple is also noteworthy in that it preserves part of the architraves and pediments. Sacrificial altars and a votive column are situated in the area in front of the building.

The remains of paleo-Christian tombs are also preserved within the temple. It should be recalled that when Paestum began to decline and the inhabitants began seeking refuge in the neighbouring hills, a small community of Christians remained behind and on several occasions adapted local buildings to their cult.

In this case too, it has to be said that the name given to this temple -that of Ceres - is incorrect: in fact, it was probably sacred to the goddess Athena, as may be deduced from surviving inscriptions and fragments of statues dedicated to her.

Paestum: aerial view of the Temple of Ceres.

THE AREA OF THE FORUM AND THE VIA SACRA

Apart from the wails and the big temples we have already described, the excavations of Paestum have also revealed a series of buildings mainly situated in the central part of the town and more particularly along the cardo, the street constituting its main north south axis. At the intersection between the cardo and the decumanus we find in fact the extensive Forum area: a series of public buildings which constituted the town's religious, political and economic centre are arranged around a square 150 metres long and 50 metres wide. It was in this area that the civic life of Paestum was concentrated and hence it was here that the town's most important buildings were built. The Roman Forum thus came to play the same role as the Greek agora (a square used as a combined market and meeting place). Here were to be found the various Temples, the Curia (the meeting-place of the senators), the Baths and the shops. Here public affairs were carried out. And it was from here that the Via Sacra started out - the street along which the most important religious buildings of the town were raised and processions held. Various buildings can still be identified in the Forum of Paestum today, but of many of them only the foundations remain. One of the most important is the Italic Temple situated close to the Theatre. It was built in the 3rd century B.C., but subsequently remodelled. It was probably dedicated to Jupiter, father of the gods. Surrounded by beautiful columns on all four sides, it was not particularly big, but raised on a high podium and approached by a flight of steps.

A stroll along the Via Sacra is also of particular interest. It was flanked by several houses and, in the vicinity of the Temple of Ceres, by a sacellum, or underground temple, probably dedicated to the goddess Hera, which is well worth visiting. The rich and varied archeological material found here is now preserved in the Museum of Paestum.

THE MUSEUM NATIONAL OF PAESTUM

Set up in 1952, the Museum is of considerable importance for our knowledge of paintings, sculpture and pottery of the Italic, Greek and Roman civilizations. In particular, it houses and displays the archeological material found during the excavations of Paestum, as well as the findings from the wonderful Sanctuary of the Argive Hera which is situated a few kilometres away and is one of the most beautiful and important complexes of its kind to have come down to us from antiquity. Many paintings and grave goods found in the various cemeteries in the area are also displayed. A visit to the Museum may thus contribute greatly to our knowledge of the art and civilization of the past. Each exhibit is clearly marked with its provenance and date to facilitate a reconstruction of the historical and artistic background. Below we give a brief review of some of the most interesting pieces. Some of the Museum's prize exhibits are a series of frescoes which once covered the walls of tombs in the area. Especially beautiful are those from the Tomb of the Diver, whose name derives from a scene represented in the paintings. Other no less interesting paintings are those from Lucanian tombs. Their subject-matter is varied: we can identify scenes of gladiatorial combat, chariot races and funeral processions with portraits of the dead. The Museum of Paestum also houses a marvellous series of metopes from the various temples of Paestum and of the Argive Hera. These are sculpted friezes which portray scenes from Greek myth and are astonishing for the power, eloquence and immediacy of their compositions. They include, for example, representations of the various battles and exploits of Hercules, and of famous episodes from the Trojan War. The Museum also contains statues, amphoras, grave goods and a beautiful collection of Greek vases.

Paestum Museum: tomb of the diver - detail of the decorations which embellish the tomb.

Caserta, a modern industrial town, has a singular history. In contrast to so many other Italian towns, its origins are comparatively modern. Its birth and importance were in fact determined by the construction of the vast Royal Palace which is also the town's most illustrious monument. Until the mid-18th century only a modest village called La Torre existed on the site, though some 10 kilometres away there was another village of ancient origins actually called Caserta. This village, which is of considerable interest for its monuments (they are described below), was later given the name of Caserta Vecchia to distinguish it from the growing modern town associated with the Bourbon Royal Palace now rechristened Caserta.

It was in fact in 1751 that work began on the construction of the Royal Palace on the site of the village of La Torre. The palace was the brainchild of Charles III of Bourbon who wished to emulate the splendour of the courts of Versailles and Potsdam. The commission for its design was assigned to Luigi Vanvitelli, a distinguished architect of the period, who fully satisfied the wishes of the monarch by creating a monumental and spectacular complex of palace and parkland. Vanvitelli directed the work - which was on a huge scale - and completed most of it within a period of 25 years, but on his death in 1773 it was continued by his son Cario who made some alterations to his father's plan.

In the meantime, king Charles III had acceded to the throne of Spain, with the result that he was prevented from seeing the completion of the palace whose building he had promoted with so much enthusiasm, or indeed of using it as his own residence. It was, however, occupied by his successor, Ferdinand IV of Bourbon, who continued work on its embellishment and surrounded himself with a splendid court which became a focal point of social and

Caserta: view of the façade of the splendid Royal Palace, designed by the architect Vanvitelli.

cultural attraction. This led to the formation of a small satellite town in the immediate proximity of the palace. The town progressively grew in both size and importance: Caserta was thus born.

The Royal Palace - the Reggia to give it its Italian name - and the beautiful park in which it is set, occupy a vast area. The palace itself is rectangular in plan (measuring roughly 250 x 200 metres) and divided internally into four parts by two orthogonally intersecting wings, thus defining four courtyards, one in each quarter. The rear façade of the palace looks onto a magnificent park which extends some 3 kilometres towards the hills to the back of Caserta.

On entering the palace - its portico supported by a hundred columns - we find ourselves in a vast octagonal hall (a masterpiece of Vanvitelli's art), from which a magnificent marble-encased staircase leads up to the Court Chapel and the Royal Apartments on the first floor. The Royal Apartments themselves - their windows overlooking the front of the palace - occupy only some thirty of the 2000 rooms comprised by the palace. Large and sumptuous in style, they are richiy decorated with paintings, sculptures and valuable furnishings. Of particular interest is the furniture, from that period mainly in the Empire Style.

The Royal Palace of Caserta, as a whole, represents the highest expression of 18th century art in Southern Italy. Imposing in its proportions, in the solemn articulation of its parts, and in its happy fusion of the spectacular effects of the baroque with the more sedate and measured canons of neoclassicism, it constitutes above all the masterpiece of Vanvitelli's art.

Above: *Throne Room.*
Below: *Council Room with the richly carved central table, donated by the City of Naples to King Francesco I on the occasion of his marriage.*

Overall view of the entrance-hall and ceremonial staircase.

THE PARK OF THE ROYAL PALACE

The marvellous garden adjoining the Royal Palace - and surely its most precious jewel - was also designed by Vanvitelli, who utilized the natural conditions of the land in laying out a series of lawns, thickets of evergreens, hedges and cypress, alleyways, fountains, cascades, bridges, basins and flights of steps extending for a distance of over 3 kilometres towards the hills to the back of Caserta.

The wonderful interplay of carefully orchestrated sounds and colours is fused into a marvellous whole. The whole vast system of basins (those of Aeolus, Ceres, the Dolphin and Venus) culminates in the magnificent Grand Cascade which descends gently between green banks to flow into the large fishpond of Diana and Actaeon where beautiful groups of statues represent the myth of the young hunter transformed into a stag for having defied the goddess.

The park also contains a beautiful English Garden: an area of lush vegetation notable for the variety of its plants. It was laid out for Queen Maria Carolina of Austria.

The water which flows into the park's several fishponds is supplied by an impressive aqueduct stretching for over 40 km; it too was designed by Vanvitelli.

The whole complex - palace, park, architecture, statuary, water and nature - is fused into an inseparable whole which makes Caserta one of the most dazzling creations of human ingenuity.

View of the Park of the Royal Palace and its splendid fountains.

CASERTA VECCHIA

Caserta Vecchia represents the original nucleus of the new Caserta which developed as a result of the Bourbon occupation of the Royal Palace. Yet it is situated some 10 km. away. We have already touched on the reasons that determined the growth of the modern town so removed from its historic counterpart and pointed out how it took its name to confirm, in some away, its ideal links with the past and its history. The old town was then designated Caserta Vecchia to distinguish it from the new one. Caserta Vecchia boasts of Lombard origins (though some scholars believe it has even more ancient origins than that). It is situated on the slopes of a hill, and its altitude is in fact connoted by its very name: Caserta is derived from "casa irta", meaning "high house". The village soon acquired some importance; it became a county. And it grew further when the inhabitants of the plain were forced to seek refuge in it as a result of various incursions.

The Bishop's residence was transferred here too and work began on the construction of the wonderful Cathedral which unequivocally testifies to the town's prestige. Begun in 1113, the Cathedral was completed by the middle of the same century. It represents an amalgam of various styles: the Romanesque, the Saracenic, the Norman and the influence of local architectural styles.

Yet apart from this Cathedral, which is undoubtedly the most prestigious monument of Caserta Vecchia, the whole town is full of other beauties. what fascinates most, however, is its atmosphere: everything seems unchanged, the solitary and winding streets, the charming little piazzas, the medieval houses - everything has retained its age-old atmosphere and appearance.

Caserta Vecchia: view of the old town of Caserta and its Cathedral.

A beautiful circle of mountains, dominated by the high peaks of Monte Terminio and Monte Partenio (better known as Monte Vergine), encloses the fertile valley in which Avellino - the ancient Abellinum - is situated. In origin it was a Samnite settlement with some economic importance. It was later occupied by the Romans, by whom the Samnite people were completely subjugated. Following the barbarian invasions and the devastation of the town by the Lombards, it was removed to a new and more fortifiable position on high ground in the vicinity, where it grew clustered round its main focal point: the Cathedral. In the course of centuries Avellino underwent various vicissitudes and domination over it was long contested by various lords. when the Bourbons became rulers of the Kingdom of Naple. Avellino became the provincial capital. Today, the town is largely modern in appearance and has expanded into the plain below. Yet the old city centre clustered round the Cathedral remains, with its own different urban characteristics: irregular streets and houses arranged in an asymmetrical fashion. A visit to the town should include the Cathedral, which dates to the 12th century but has undergone considerable alterations in later periods (particularly beautiful are its wooden choir stalls), the church of Santa Maria di Costantinopoli and the nearby 17th century fountain, and the Museo Irpino (with a wealth of archeological material from the Irpina area). Avellino can also boast of its beautiful environs. Recommended excursions include that to Montevergine. Here, splendidly situated amid an unforgettable landscape, lies the famous Sanctuary of Montevergine, a muchloved place for pilgrimages. It was founded in the early years of the 12th century by the Benedictine St. William of Vercelli who gathered a circle of disciples round him and instituted a monastic community on this lonely site high up in the mountains. The Sanctuary consists of a huge complex of buildings, including the Basilica, the Monastery, a Library and a Museum. The relics of the Saint are preserved in the crypt of the church. The Sanctuary is enriched with many valuable works of painting and sculpture.

BENEVENTO

The town's name (Beneventum means "good fortune") is in itself a reminder of a key turning-point in its history. It was in fact so rechristened by the Romans as a pledge of an auspicious future for a town which had hitherto been known under a name with quite the opposite connotation: Maleventum, meaning "bad fortune". And indeed up to the year 275 B.C. this Campanian town had hardly brought luck to the Roman armies, who had suffered defeat at the hands of the Samnites in a battle fought nearby. And Maleventum - or to give it is Samnite name, Maloentum - constituted a real bulwark of this tenacious people. It became the theatre of a war from which the Romans emerged victorious. And this victory naturally represented for the Romans a good omen such as to justify a change in the town's name. Thus Beneventum, thanks to the events of which it became the theatre and its geographical position (the Via Appia from Rome to Brindisi passed through it), always retained, under Roman rule, a key strategic role, and this ensured it in turn considerable political, economic and cultural importance. Today Benevento is a modern industrial town. It now extends down to the plain between the Calore and Sabato rivers and even beyond them. But testimonies to its illustrious past still remain in the older part of the town.

In fact, important remains of successive epochs in its history are still to be seen: from those dating back to the ancient Samnite settlement to those of the Roman and later the Lombard town. Yet it is the Roman period that is most widely and most richly represented. It is testified by the Theatre, the Roman Bridge and Trajan's Triumphal Arch, undoubtedly one of the most beautiful and best preserved that amtiquity has bequeathed to us.

Benevento: Trajan's Arch was built in Imperial Roman times in honour of Trajan and the opening of the Appian Way.